VICTORIOUS END-TIME CHURCH

TRUE THEOLOGY VOLUME II

JUSTIN PERRY

MorningStar Publications

The Victorious End-Time Church
By Justin Perry

©2020 1st Printing

MorningStar Ministries, Fort Mill, SC. All rights reserved.

**Distributed by MorningStar Publications, Inc.,
a division of MorningStar Fellowship Church
375 Star Light Drive, Fort Mill, Sc 29715**

**www.MorningStarMinistries.org
1-800-542-0278**

Cover design: Carlie McKinley
Layout design: Kandi Evans

ISBN: 978-1-60708-673-4
For a free catalog of MorningStar Resources, please call 1-800-542-0278

TABLE OF CONTENTS

SECTION I:

THE SPIRT & THE COMING KINGDOM

CHAPTER 1

THE SPIRIT AND THE KINGDOM

The Spirit and the Kingdom

The Day of Pentecost was the transitional moment in human history. The Spirit of God was poured out on His people to inaugurate them as a different kind of humanity. According to Acts 1:8, the power of the Spirit was given to these people so they could be God's witnesses. This means that their lives would represent and reveal Him to the earth. Their lives would testify that God and His kingdom are near or "at hand" (see Mark 1:15).

The Spirit-filled church is meant to be a community of "kingdom people"—representatives of the kingdom of God. To appreciate our identity as kingdom people, we must have a basic understanding of what the Scriptures mean by "kingdom of God." The biblical teaching of the kingdom of God is usually interpreted in one of two ways. First, the kingdom of God may refer to God's authority and dominion over the kingdoms and powers of this age (see Matthew 12:28; Mark 9:1; Luke 10:8-11). Second, the kingdom of God may refer to a future age in which Jesus will reign bodily as King over all creation (see Mark 14:24-25; Luke 13:28-29, 22:28-30). Whichever of these interpretations is correct, as kingdom people we somehow disclose God's kingdom (either His present authority or His future kingship) to the earth.

The Authority of the King and the Age of His Dominion

It seems there is significant biblical evidence for both of the above kingdom of God interpretations, and both are valid. The kingdom of God refers to His power and authority in this age *and* His literal reign in the age to come. Further, it is clear from Scripture that the kingdom of God manifests *by* His Spirit and *through* His people.

The Holy Spirit enables God's people to exercise His dominion over the powers of this age *and* to bring the age to come into our present day. When Jesus commissioned His followers to "preach the kingdom of God" and "heal the sick, cleanse the lepers, raise the dead, and cast out demons" (see Matthew 10:7-8; Luke 9:2, 10:9), He made a connection between the nearness of the kingdom of God and the miraculous powers believers are called to walk in. In other words, the presence of the kingdom of God manifests through His people in the gifts of the Holy Spirit.

Jesus' first-century audience would have been acutely sensitive to His language of the imminence of the kingdom of God. They were waiting for the kingdom of God to come (see Luke 23:51). To them, Jesus meant that Messiah would soon come to set up the kingdom of God on the earth. He would vanquish their enemies, throw off Roman political oppression, become their king, and initiate a new age of the presence of God on the earth. For Jesus to say **"the kingdom of God is at hand" (see Mark 1:15)** meant that the defeat of their enemies and reign of God on the earth was about to begin. Further for Him to say, **"If I cast out demons by the Spirit of God, surely the kingdom of *God has come upon you"* (see Matthew 12:28)** meant that the reign of God on the earth had already begun through Him. They would have understood Jesus to mean, "The age to come, which you have been waiting for, is already here. I have brought a manifestation of the age to come into the present moment."

An Eschatological People

Jesus gave His followers simple instructions. His commission to the seventy was the same as His commission to the twelve: *perform miraculous signs by the Spirit of God and preach the imminence of His kingdom* (see Matthew 10, Luke 9-10). His commission to believers today is no different. When we walk in the power of the Spirit, we announce the coming of His kingdom. We walk in dominion over the powers of this age because, by the Spirit, we impose the powers of the age to come into the present day. In this sense, we are an "eschatological people" who bring the future into the present. Eschatology is the "study of last things" or the theology of the future.

In Gordon Fee's excellent book, *Paul, the Spirit, and the People of God,* he expounds on the identity of the church as an eschatological people. Fee explains that the Holy Spirit "enables us to live as a radically eschatological people in the present world, while we await the consummation [of the ages]. All the rest, including fruit and gifts [of the Spirit] . . . serve to that end." Fee goes on to explain that this is the primary reason the Spirit of God has been given to the church—to inaugurate us as an "eschatological people."

Spirit-filled believers live in the present age as citizens of the age to come. We walk in authority over sickness because in the age to come, there is no sickness. We walk in authority over demons because in the age to come, demons have no dominion. We carry the presence of God because in the age to come, the presence of God dominates the atmosphere. The Spirit upon us manifests the kingdom of God in this present age.

In the proceeding chapters, we will examine many glorious characteristics of the coming kingdom of God. To the degree that we walk as kingdom people by the power of the Holy Spirit, we will demonstrate these characteristics—in the present age. The Spirit makes us faithful witnesses of Jesus, the King, and the reality of His kingdom.

Morning Star

In Scripture there is a prophetic picture that illustrates these realities—the Morning Star. Throughout antiquity, the Morning Star was an astronomical indicator of time. For thousands of years, men measured time by the position of the sun during the day and the position of the stars at night. Therefore, late in the darkness of night, the Morning Star would rise over the horizon and announce to the earth "the night is coming to an end and a new day is dawning."

The prophetic significance of this phenomenon is that the Morning Star is not a star, it is the planet Venus. As a planet, Venus has no light of its own; it merely reflects the light of the coming sun. In Scripture, the church is promised to display the characteristics of the Morning Star in two passages (see II Peter 1:19; Revelation 2:28). Further, in the Word of God, the sun is often a picture of Jesus, the Son of God (see Malachi 4:2; II Samuel 23:4) and the sun shining above the earth is a picture of the Son (the King) reigning over His kingdom.

As the church steps into the Morning Star identity, we begin to shine brightly in the midst of the night. We reflect the glory of the Son who is coming, and our very lives announce that the night is ending and a new day is breaking forth. Where we go, the sick are healed and the oppressed are delivered as a witness to the King and His coming kingdom. We walk in the fulfillment of the prayer Jesus taught us, **"Father, Your kingdom come. Your will be done on earth as it is in heaven" (see Matthew 6:9-10).**

May we walk in the power of the Holy Spirit and bring the age to come into our present day!

CHAPTER 2
THE PEOPLE
OF GOD

The Age Between the Ages

L iving in the church age has been compared to living in Europe between D-Day and V-Day. On June 6, 1944 (D-Day), Allied forces broke through Nazi resistance, ensuring ultimate victory. However, it was not until May 8, 1945 (V-Day) that World War II finally ended. There were many battles during the interim, but the outcome had all but been decided. In the same way, we are living in "the age between the ages." The age of Satan's dominion, in a real sense, ended at the death and resurrection of Jesus. However, the full manifestation of Jesus' victory will not be realized until His second coming and the inauguration of a new age: The kingdom of God on the earth.

This "age between the ages" is often referred to as the *eschaton,* or the end times. Peter preached in Acts 2 that the beginning of the *eschaton* coincided with the outpouring of the Holy Spirit at Pentecost. He also explained that the outpouring of the Spirit was accompanied by prophecy, dreams, visions, signs and wonders, mass salvation, and that these supernatural occurrences are evidence that the day of the Lord is approaching (see Acts 2:17-21). Those who receive the outpouring of the

Holy Spirit and begin to walk in His supernatural manifestation become evidence to the earth of a shift in the ages.

In the last chapter we examined the role of the Holy Spirit in the life of the believer, specifically in manifesting the kingdom of God. We will continue this study of the Holy Spirit and how He brings the future into our present day.

The Presence of the Future

The scholarly works of George Eldon Ladd were a breath of fresh air in the middle of the 20th century. Christian academia was heavily influenced by liberal scholarship and many evangelicals spurned the academy rather than entering into dialogue. G.E. Ladd responded to the need of the hour by writing anointed scholarly works as a committed evangelical theologian. His *The Presence of the Future* proved to be an important work for academia as well as for the Spirit-filled church. Ladd's writings became a major influence in evangelicalism and significant ministries such as John Wimber's.

The thesis of *The Presence of the Future* is simple: by the Holy Spirit, believers live in the "already/not yet" experience of the kingdom of God. There is a future reality of the kingdom that will come with unrestrained power at the second coming of Christ, but by the Spirit of God we can manifest this future age into our present moment. We *already* have access to the power and glory of the age to come in measure, but we have *not yet* received their fullness. We are truly an eschatological people—a people of the future who live as witnesses of the coming King and His kingdom.

Jesus taught us to pray, **"Your kingdom come. Your will be done on earth as it is in heaven" (see Matthew 6:10).** In Jesus' thinking, we should be those who bring the future kingdom of God into our present day. He also taught us to pray, "Give us this day tomorrow's bread" (from the Greek *epiousios artos* in Matthew 6:11). This Greek phrase *epiousios artos* is rendered "daily bread" in many translations but is often footnoted as "tomorrow's bread." In the context of Matthew 6:10-11, it makes the most sense that Jesus is telling us to pray that we would receive tomorrow's bread (the substance of His *future* kingdom), today.

The Power of the Holy Spirit

The work of the Holy Spirit in our lives distinguishes us as a people from another kingdom. It is evident as a person walks in miraculous healing or prophetic revelation that they are different from their neighbors. A person who presses through the tide of immorality and self-indulgence, who displays uncompromising character, becomes a spectacle to their generation.

The fruit of the Holy Spirit differentiates us as a revolutionary kind of humanity. We manifest virtues counter to the disposition of the world, revealing the character of the coming kingdom. According to Jesus, the world will know we are His when they see our love (see John 13:35). He also said that He would give us a peace that is unlike any worldly peace (see John 14:27) and a joy that nothing in the world can steal from us (see John 16:22). Jesus spoke these things in the context of preparing His disciples for His departure and the coming of the Holy Spirit. The Spirit at work in our lives produces the other-worldly characteristics of: love, joy, peace, patience, kindness, goodness, faithfulness, gentleness, and self-control (see Galatians 5:22-24).

Paul makes it clear that the power of the Spirit is given to us for **"the profit of all" (see I Corinthians 12:7).** This means that the gifts of the Holy Spirit are essential tools, given to benefit all mankind. They are manifestations of the power of the kingdom of God, revealing the superiority of the age to come and temporality of the present age. The world needs believers to walk in supernatural words of wisdom and knowledge, prophetic revelation, and miraculous healing power. These supernatural demonstrations profit the world by providing the wisdom, knowledge, revelation, and power of God that humanity desperately needs. They benefit the world by giving testimony to the veracity of God and ultimately leading lives to Him.

The People of God

The Day of Pentecost (circa 33 A.D.) was a commemorative event. Jews from all over the Roman Empire gathered in Jerusalem to praise God for giving them the law, His Holy Word, fifteen hundred years earlier. They celebrated God's thunderous and fiery descent on Mount Sinai and His invitation to them to **"be a special treasure to Me above all people . . . a kingdom of priests and a holy nation" (see Exodus 19:5-6).**

The day at Sinai fifteen hundred years earlier, God expressed His desire for all 2.5 million Hebrews to be priests and holy people. As priests, they would live their lives in communion with God and minister to all of humanity from the overflow of their relationship with Him. A primary meaning of holy is "other-than" or different and separate from all others. As holy people, Israel would stand out as different from everyone else.

In Exodus 20, we read of Israel's response to God's invitation at Sinai:

All the people witnessed the thunderings, the lightning flashes, the sound of the trumpet, and

the mountain smoking; and when the people saw it, they trembled and stood afar off.

Then they said to Moses, "You speak with us, and we will hear; but let not God speak with us, lest we die."

So the people stood afar off, but Moses drew near the thick darkness where God was (Exodus 20:18-19, 21).

They stood afar off and told Moses they did not want God to speak with them personally. They sent Moses to draw near to God as a priest on their behalf. This was a definite departure from God's purpose in inaugurating them as a nation of priests, but He did not give up on His plan to have a holy people.

God gave them the law, commanding them to eat certain foods, observe special days, even shave their beards a particular way. This law ensured that they would be a different, holy people. He instituted a strict religious system, complete with a priesthood and tabernacle, ensuring that they would be a nation who represented God and His kingdom to the earth.

The People of the Kingdom

As Jews filled the temple in Jerusalem on Pentecost morning 33 A.D., they began to praise God for their identity as His people and for the gift of His Word. They corporately read Exodus 19-20 about the fire and the thunderous sounds at Sinai. They also read the customary passage from Ezekiel 1 about God coming in the whirlwind full of fire.

Suddenly, a shocking sound roared through the city. It was a sound like a mighty rushing wind, so dramatic that thousands ran to discover the source of the commotion (see Acts 2:6). As they gathered in front of the Upper Room, they were astonished to see the fulfillment of what God intended fifteen hundred years earlier at Mount Sinai. Before them was a company of people with supernatural fire resting on their heads. Every one of them was speaking the Word of God (see Acts 2:11) in a language which could be understood by all nationalities. The Holy Spirit had been poured out on one hundred twenty people, and they were living demonstrations of the fire, wind, and Word of God which was prophesied in Scripture. Only this time, God had not descended on a mountain, He had descended on His people.

Peter stood and explained the spectacle they were witnessing. Before their very eyes, God was inaugurating a people to be His special treasure in the earth. A kingdom of priests was being born, a holy people, utterly different and marked by the power of His presence. Peter preached that Jesus of Nazareth, whom they had crucified, was their King, their long-awaited Messiah, and that **"God raised Him up again, putting an end to the agony of death, since it was impossible for Him to be held in its power"(Acts 2:24 NAS)**. He declared that it was through faith in the resurrected Jesus that these one hundred twenty had been born into the kingdom of God and received the Holy Spirit.

Peter's hearers were **"cut to the heart"** and cried out, **"'What shall we do?' Then Peter said to them, 'Repent, and let every one of you be baptized in the name of Jesus Christ for the remission of sins; and you shall receive the gift of the Holy Spirit'" (see Acts 2:37-38).** Many responded in faith and were born into the kingdom of God that day. At Sinai, three thousand people died under the power of the law (see Exodus 32:28), but on this Pentecost morning three thousand received new life in the power of the Spirit. **"The** [Law] **kills, but the Spirit gives life" (see II Corinthians 3:6).**

Since that day nearly two thousand years ago, millions of people have received the gift of the Spirit. The people of God have spread to the four corners of the earth. We are citizens of the age to come, the people of His kingdom. May we walk as faithful witnesses of the King, revealing Him to the world by the Holy Spirit. May we live as priests of God, holy people, His special treasure.

CHAPTER 3

THE VICTORIOUS END-TIME CHURCH

Darkness and Glory

Diamonds are often set against black cloth to display their glory. In the same way, the glory of the end-time church is best appreciated when seen against the backdrop of end-time tribulation. It is true that **"darkness will cover the earth, and deep darkness the people,"** but we must remember that God's **"glory will appear upon"** those who are His **(see Isaiah 60:2 NAS).**

Understanding the glory of the end-time church and the culmination of the last-day plan of God is critically important. We must study the "bad news" of end-time prophecy in light of the "good news" that appears in the midst. It is only as we understand the glory of the end-time church and second coming of Jesus that our hearts are equipped to study eschatological tribulation.

In the previous two chapters we examined the empowerment of the Holy Spirit, an important facet of pneumatology. In the Scriptures, pneumatology is inseparably linked with eschatology, the study of last things, or the end-times. We will now begin to explore God's glorious plan for the culmination of the ages.

A Time of Trouble Like the World has Never Seen

Matthew 24-25 contains "The Olivet Discourse," Jesus' most extensive eschatological statement. In Matthew 24:3, the disciples asked Him three questions, **"When will these things be? And what will be the sign of Your coming, and of the end of the age?"** The first question referred to Jesus' prophecy in Matthew 24:1 about the destruction of the temple. The next two questions pertained to the return of Christ and the culmination of the ages, which the disciples assumed would coincide with the destruction of the temple. Jesus goes into a lengthy discourse in answer to these questions. He speaks of many negative global events that will take place in a contracted span of time preceding His coming. It appears from history that the destruction of the temple by Titus in 70 A.D. was a localized foreshadowing of the "great tribulation" to come. Thus, Jesus prophetically answered all three of the disciples' questions at the same time.

Jesus touches on several significant eschatological themes in His answers to these questions. The first theme He illuminates is **"the beginning of sorrows" (see Matthew 24:8)**, a period of significant trouble the world will endure. During this time, there will be great deception, war, famine, and earthquakes. This season of trouble sounds severe, but Jesus explains that it is merely **"the beginning."** This is a time preceding the great tribulation, which will bring sorrow upon the world because of the intensely negative events. Many have debated whether the church will be here for the tribulation. However, regardless of the timing of the rapture, the church will certainly be on earth during the difficulty of the **"beginning of sorrows."**

The next eschatological theme Jesus discusses is the **"great tribulation, such as has not been since the beginning of the world" (see Matthew 24:21).** He warns His followers to flee Judea when they see **"the abomination of desolation, spoken of by Daniel the prophet" (see Matthew 24:15),** which will mark the beginning of this time of tribulation. He then goes on to explain that this time of tribulation will be so traumatic that everyone on earth would be killed if it were not kept short. He describes the false religion that will spread globally with signs, wonders, and claims of a secret coming of Christ, and He warns His followers not to be deceived. He concludes with a declaration that His coming will flash across the sky like lightning—it will not be secret.

After portraying the great tribulation, Jesus describes His second coming, another important end-time theme. He begins with these words,

> *Immediately after the tribulation of those days* **the sun will be darkened, and the moon will not give its light; the stars will fall from heaven, and the powers of the heavens will be shaken.**
>
> **Then the sign of the Son of Man will appear in heaven, and then all the tribes of the earth will mourn, and they will see the Son of Man coming on the clouds of heaven with power and great glory.**
>
> **And He will send His angels with a great sound of a trumpet, and they will gather together His elect from the four winds (see Matthew 24:29-31).**

This passage is a clear description of the second coming of Jesus. There will be supernatural phenomena that will appear in the sky and **"all the tribes of the earth . . . will see the Son of Man coming on the clouds of heaven."** At that time, He will send His angels with the sound of a trumpet and they will gather the elect to Him—as He comes on the clouds of heaven (this event is often referred to as the rapture).

It seems that this passage plainly answers the question of the timing of Jesus' second coming and the rapture of the church. Jesus says that these events (His coming and the rapture) take place **"immediately *after the tribulation* of those days."** Since He has just finished speaking of the great tribulation, it is reasonable to assume Jesus is speaking of a post-tribulation rapture.

The implications of this are immense. If the rapture takes place after the great tribulation, then the church will be on the earth for the most intense time of trouble that the world has ever known. The questions must be asked, "What will this time be like for the church? Will we be overcome in the tumult of trouble, or will we thrive? Will the tribulation be the worst time of our earthly lives, or will it be our greatest hour?"

A People of Power Like the World has Never Seen

There is debate about the nature of the "abomination of desolation" of which Jesus and Daniel spoke. It is clear, however, from Daniel 11 and Matthew 24 that this abomination is set up during the end-time tribulation by an evil ruler (many would agree that this is the antichrist). The antichrist will wage war against the saints of God and even kill some in persecution. However, Daniel 11:32 tells us that at the very time this evil ruler is setting up his abomination, **"the people who know their God shall be strong, and carry out great exploits."** The people of God will be walking in great demonstrations of His power during the times of tribulation.

Like the bride in Song of Solomon, **"coming up from the wilderness leaning on her beloved" (see Song of Solomon**

8:5), the church prevails in tribulation as she leans on the Lord in unequivocal faith. Even the persecution of Daniel 11 serves to purify the saints of God, to refine them, and make them white (see Daniel 11:35). Ephesians 5:27 makes it clear that end-time believers will be **"a glorious church, not having spot or wrinkle or any such thing, but that she should be holy and without blemish."** This is why the end-time church is described as a **"bride"** who **"has made herself ready" (see Revelation 19:7 ESV).** As a bride prepares herself for the wedding day, Jesus' bride, the church, is purified in preparation for His coming. These purified saints will walk in supernatural wisdom from God and will influence many people (see Daniel 11:33). Jesus referred to these empowered end-time saints as **"the sons of the kingdom"** who **"will shine forth as the sun"** during the time of the **"harvest** [at] **the end of the age" (see Matthew 13:36-43).**

Indeed, this great harvest Jesus spoke of in Matthew 13:39 will culminate during the end-time tribulation. Revelation 14:14-20 gives us a vivid picture of this harvest. Jesus is seated on a cloud with a crown on His head and a sickle in His hand. He swings the sickle to reap His harvest of souls, the **"sons of the kingdom."** Next, a great angel comes from heaven with a sickle in his hand. He swings the sickle to reap the harvest of wickedness from the earth, to throw it into the winepress for the wrath of God. The time of harvest is **"the fullness of time" (see Ephesians 1:10),** when all the seeds mankind has sown throughout history come to fruition. Seeds of righteousness are reaped as an ingathering of souls and an outpouring of the Holy Spirit. The seeds of wickedness are reaped **"when transgressors have reached their fullness" (see Daniel 8:23)** and God judges the unrepentant sins of six thousand years of hman history. The Apostle Paul gives us a vivid description of the "fullness" of transgression:

But know this, that in the last days perilous times will come:

For men will be lovers of themselves, lovers of money, boasters, proud, blasphemers, disobedient to parents, unthankful, unholy,

unloving, unforgiving, slanderers, without self-control, brutal, despisers of good,

traitors, headstrong, haughty, lovers of pleasure rather than lovers of God (II Timothy 3:1-4).

Joel 2 and Acts 2 both promise an outpouring of the Spirit on God's people in the last days. As previously observed, this began on the Day of Pentecost, but will increase and culminate before Jesus' return to earth. This last-day outpouring of the Spirit comes with prophecy, dreams, visions, signs, and wonders (see Acts 2:17-19). Those who receive this outpouring preach a powerful message: The Gospel of the Kingdom (see Matthew 9:35). This Spirit-empowered proclamation and demonstration of God's soon-coming kingdom will go to the ends of the earth before the end of this age (see Matthew 24:14).

Amos 9:11-13 prophesies that the tabernacle of David will be restored at this time. Many believe this refers to a 24-7 prayer and worship movement in the Spirit of the tabernacle of David. This global increase of prayer and worship will so influence the atmosphere of cities and nations that multitudes will be awakened and come to salvation. Amos describes the intensity of this awakening in terms of unprecedented acceleration. **"Behold, the days are coming," says the LORD, "When the plowman shall overtake the reaper, and the treader of grapes him who sows seed" (Amos 9:13).** This vivid language describes an explosive harvest where the seeds instantly come to maturity and are harvested the moment they are sown. Amos further tells us that the Holy Spirit is poured out during this harvest as "sweet wine" and God's people will "possess" or lead to salvation "Edom and all the nations." This will be a historic outpouring and ingathering!

We know from John 14:12 that before Jesus returns there will be a people on earth who perform all the supernatural works He walked in and even "greater works." The works of Jesus include opening blind eyes and deaf ears, multiplication of food, turning water into wine, raising the dead, walking on water, and more. His people will do all these things and more. They will manifest great healing power in the last days as "the Sun of Righteousness rises with healing in His wings" (see Malachi 4:1-2). Further, we read in Micah 7:8-17 of a time in the future when God will dramatically act on behalf of His people. He will do the same miracles for them which He did when He brought Israel out of Egypt, and all nations of the earth will take notice. This means He will give food from heaven, water from rocks, and visible manifestations of the glory of God. It also means He will supernaturally judge the enemies of His people.

It is evident from end-time prophecy that the antichrist will have a political, military, religious, and economic empire (see Daniel 7 and 11; Revelation 13 and 17). Those who choose to be a part of his system will have access to his resources, and those who refuse to accept his leadership will be cut off from them (Revelation 13:16-17). However, those who reject the leadership of the antichrist will have access to the resources of heaven. They will have access to the limitless power of the Holy Spirit and all the miracles God performed when He brought Israel out of Egypt!

Goshen, in the Exodus narrative, was a prophetic foreshadowing of the last-day church. As God poured out judgment on Pharaoh's kingdom, Goshen was impacted in measure. However, after the third plague, Goshen was fully protected from the effects of the judgment being released. It is a striking illustration for us to imagine that even as darkness completely covered the land of Egypt, there was light shining down from heaven, illuminating the entire city of Goshen.

In the same way, as God pours out judgment on the antichrist (the end-time Pharaoh) and his evil empire, darkness will indeed cover the earth. However, in the midst of that darkness, the glory of God will shine on His people and be seen upon them. The glory that rests on His people will cause multitudes to come into the kingdom of God—nations, kings, sons, and daughters (see Isaiah 60:1-4). The New Testament portrays the end-time church as **"blameless and harmless, children of God without fault in the midst of a crooked and perverse generation, among whom you shine as lights in the world" (see Philippians 2:15).** The most traumatic time of tribulation the earth has ever known will be the greatest hour for the church. **"Then** [we] **shall see and become radiant, and [our] heart shall swell with joy!" (see Isaiah 60:5).**

The End of the Age and Beginning of the Kingdom

As Rick Joyner has often said, "It is through many tribulations that we enter the kingdom of God, and it is through the great tribulation that the whole earth enters the age of the kingdom" (see Acts 14:22). Jesus told us to rejoice when we see the signs of tribulation coming upon the earth because it means that our redemption is drawing near (see Luke 21:28). As Christians, we do not believe in the "end of the world," only the end of this age. The end of this age is the beginning of the age of the kingdom of God. Therefore, let us rejoice that His kingdom is coming.

We were born for "such a time as this." God has uniquely created end-time believers to live in the most turbulent times the earth has ever known. If we are not given the opportunity to walk through such times, we will never step into the fullness of power and potential we were made for. Soon we will have this opportunity, and the world will see the victorious end-time church.

CHAPTER 4

THE COMING OF THE KING

The Ancient of Days and the Son of Man

The vision in Daniel 7:9-14 contains one of the most epic scenes in all of Scripture. The Father is seen as the Ancient of Days, seated on His fiery throne, with billions of souls worshipping before Him in heaven. Next, the vision pans down to earth, and Daniel sees the final moments of this age, the battle of Armageddon. As Daniel "kept looking," the vision pans back to heaven and he sees the Son of Man come before the throne, riding on the clouds of heaven. The Ancient of Days gives to Him, **"dominion and glory and a kingdom, that all peoples, nations, and languages should serve Him. His dominion is an everlasting dominion."** In this vision Daniel sees the moments in heaven just before Jesus returns to earth.

In second coming passages, we are told Jesus will return to earth from heaven, riding on the clouds (see Matthew 24:30-31; I Thessalonians 4:16-17; Acts 1:9-11). In Daniel 7:13-14, Jesus is riding on the clouds of heaven, being given dominion over all peoples and nations by the Father, preparing to enter the earth-realm to challenge His adversaries.

In chapter three, we beheld the victorious end-time church, an important eschatological motif. In this chapter, we will examine the second coming of Jesus, the most important eschatological event and the great future hope of the New Testament.

Earth's Precarious Condition

As we previously observed, the last days are the most intense times the world will ever know. History reaches a point of critical mass, or to use the language of Scripture, a harvest. All the seeds of righteousness that have been sown will come to fruition and be reaped; massive numbers of people will come to faith in Jesus in a great move of God (see Matthew 13:24-30, 36-39; Revelation 14:14-16). Concurrently, all the seeds of iniquity that have been sown will mature and culminate in a season of wickedness rivaled only by the days of Noah (see Matthew 24:37; Genesis 6:5-6). This harvest of wickedness will invoke the judgment of God, and He will respond with great wrath (see Revelation 14:17-20).

Revelation 17:4 paints a vivid picture of the spiritual condition of the nations of the earth during the time preceding Christ's coming. An angel shows John the great harlot, **"arrayed in purple and scarlet, and adorned with gold and precious stones and pearls, having in her hand a golden cup full of abominations and the filthiness of her fornication."** Harlotry in Scripture represents false religion or apostasy. It is when mankind forsakes God (her true husband) and chases many other lovers (false gods and religions). The kings and inhabitants of the earth have committed adultery with the great harlot and they have become drunk with the wine of her cup (see Revelation 17:2). The harlot **"sits on many waters" (see Revelation 17:1),** which signifies her influence over many people and nations. The masses of humanity will partake of this apostate religion.

The harlot's wine is a blend of three intoxicants: fornication (see Revelation 17:2), abominations (see Revelation 17:4), and the blood of the saints and martyrs (see Revelation 17:6)—her false religion features all three elements. One hallmark of end-time apostasy is *fornication*—all sorts of sexual sins are acceptable. Moral lines are blurred and living by "what feels right to you" is encouraged. Another hallmark of this harlot-spirituality is *abomination*, the worship of other gods. "Religious tolerance" rules the day and "finding your own path to God" is celebrated. It is arrogant for one to assume they have found "the only way to heaven" and such "narrowmindedness" is condemned. These two hallmarks provoke a collision with the prophetic church and the result is martyrdom, *the blood of the saints*. The saints speak out against the harlot and resist her poisonous wine, some even unto death.

The harlot is in partnership with the beast (the antichrist); she rides on his back. There are fascinating elements of this partnership that we do not have room to examine here. However, as we discover from Daniel 7 and 9, Revelation 13, and Revelation 17-18, the beast dominates the world through a political, military, religious, and economic empire. The ultimate result of this domination is world-wide war, famine, pestilence, and death (see Revelation 6:3-8).

As we discovered in our previous study, the victorious end-time church thrives in the midst of these difficult times. However, the end-time harvest of wickedness is prevalent all over the world. All of creation is groaning for a King-Savior to come and impose His kingdom onto the earth.

Christ's Messianic Resolution

Just as Daniel 7 gives us insight into the *final moments* in heaven just prior to the second coming, the Book of Revelation portrays many events in heaven during the *final years* before Jesus' return.

Revelation 4-5 is the premier throne room scene in the Scriptures, giving us more detail about this heavenly location than any other passage. There are many glorious realities in these chapters, but we will focus only on a few.

Revelation 5:1 introduces a scroll in the **"right hand of Him who sat on the throne . . . sealed with seven seals."** This scroll is obviously reminiscent of the scroll Daniel was given and told to **"seal . . . until the time of the end" (see Daniel 12:4)**. In fact, we discover in the next chapter of Revelation that this is the scroll Daniel saw, which initiates "the time of the end" as it is opened.

In Revelation 5:2-3, a search is made in all of heaven and earth, even under the earth, for one who is worthy to open the scroll and release its monumental power. Each seal of this all-important scroll will release historic events and traumatic judgments—who could be entrusted with this outstanding power?

Almost at the point of despairing that no suitable person will be found, a heavenly elder reveals the only One who is worthy: **"Behold, the Lion of the tribe of Judah, the Root of David, has prevailed to open the scroll and to loose its seven seals" (see Revelation 5:5)**. When John turns to look at this Lion, he sees Him as **"a Lamb as though it had been slain . . . Then He came and took the scroll out of the right hand of Him who sat on the throne" (see Revelation 5:6-7)**. All of heaven begins to rejoice that Jesus has taken the scroll and will open its seals. **"And they sang a new song, saying: 'You are worthy to take the scroll, and to open its seals; for You were slain, and have redeemed us to God by Your blood'" (Revelation 5:9).**

This becomes a major interpretive key for the entire Book of Revelation. In the proceeding chapters, the most terrifying judgments are propagated on mankind, and Jesus is seen as the one in charge of releasing them. However, Jesus does not present Himself as Judge while releasing the judgments, nor even as Conquering King. As Mike Bickle highlights in his *Book of Revelation Study Guide*, Jesus presents Himself as the Lamb who was slain to redeem humanity. It is Jesus in His identity as the Savior, Healer, and Redeemer who opens the seals and initiates "the time of the end."

This is why He is the only one worthy to take the scroll. He has always had the power to destroy rebellious mankind, yet He chose to be destroyed on their behalf. He would have been just in condemning the human race, but He instead satisfied the justice of the Father at Calvary for us. The Lion, who is also the slain Lamb, is the one who opens the seals and releases their power.

From this point forward in the Book of Revelation we must realize that each judgment we see is for the purpose of salvation. God is looking for mankind to repent so that He can redeem them. This is evidenced in several places where we are told, "they did not repent" in response to the judgments (see Revelation 9:20, 21; 16:9, 11). Even the seemingly severe events of the Book of Revelation are saving acts of Jesus. They are for the purpose of bringing men to repentance and salvation, and they are in response to the wickedness expounded in the section above.

The Trumpet and the Coming of the King

In many "second coming" passages in the New Testament, we see the blast of a trumpet accompanying the coming of Jesus (see Matthew 24:31; I Corinthians 15:52; I Thessalonians 4:16). I Corinthians 15 is one of the most detailed passages concerning the coming of Christ and the resurrection of the saints. Verse 52 specifies that it is the "last trumpet" which signals the coming of Christ and subsequent resurrection. Jesus returns at the sound of the "last trumpet."

The last trumpet we find in Scripture is the seventh trumpet in the Book of Revelation. It is said of the seventh trumpet, **"when he is about to sound, the mystery of God would be finished, as He declared to His servants the prophets" (see Revelation 10:7).** The mystery spoken of here, which has been declared to the prophets, is the coming of the King to establish the kingdom of God on the earth. When the seventh trumpet finally sounds, loud voices in heaven make these proclamations:

> **Then the seventh angel sounded: And there were loud voices in heaven, saying, "The kingdoms of this world have become the *kingdoms* of our Lord and of His Christ, and He shall reign forever and ever!"**
>
> **And the twenty-four elders who sat before God on their thrones fell on their faces and worshiped God,**
>
> **saying: "We give You thanks, O Lord God Almighty, The One who is and who was and who is to come, Because You have taken Your great power and reigned.**
>
> **"The nations were angry, and Your wrath has come, and the time of the dead, that they should be judged, and that You should reward Your servants the prophets and the saints, and those who fear**

Your name, small and great, and should destroy those who destroy the earth" (Revelation 11:15-18).

At the sounding of the seventh trumpet, the kingdoms of this world become **"the kingdoms of our Lord and of His Christ."** This is because the King comes at the sound of this trumpet and begins to reign with His great power. Further, at His coming, His people receive their reward (resurrected bodies) and He prepares to destroy (in the coming battle of Megiddo) those who have wrought destruction in the earth.

He is the King of Kings

Let us return to the vision of Daniel 7:9-14. As Daniel watches the Son of Man being crowned King over the nations by the Ancient of Days, he looks down to the earth and sees the final moments of the battle of Megiddo or Armageddon. The beast (the antichrist) is slain and cast into the lake of fire (see also Revelation 19:20) and the other "beasts" (global leaders in partnership with him) are defeated but kept alive, apparently for an impending time of judgment.

Earlier in Daniel 7 we read of various beast-kingdoms, or antichrist regimes throughout history. Each of the kings discussed here dominated civilization in their own day. The vision of Jesus being given authority over all earthly kingdoms, including the defeat of the last beast-king on the earth, declares something to us: Jesus Christ is the King of kings! He is exalted above every king there has ever been and He will triumph in the end.

And so, we yearn for the coming of the King. After all, He will return at the behest of His queen. It's the earnest longing of the Spirit-empowered bride that hastens His return (see II Peter

3:2). There is an eager expectation on the part of any bride and bridegroom leading up to the wedding day, the consummation of their betrothal. Jesus is eager to be eternally wed as well: **"as the bridegroom rejoices over the bride, So shall your God rejoice over you" (see Isaiah 62:5).** From now until that great wedding day, **"the Spirit and the Bride cry come" (see Revelation 22:17). "Amen. Even so, come, Lord Jesus! (see Revelation 22:20)**

CHAPTER 5

THE BATTLE FOR THE KINGDOM

Prolegomenon to Armageddon

Enthralling events precede the battle of Armageddon. We observe insanity as earthly kings challenge the Almighty Jesus and His army to battle (see Psalm 2). Revelation 16:13-16 reveals that it is not mere madness that draws the nations to Armageddon, but demonic deception. Spirits like frogs come out of the beast's and false prophet's mouths as they speak, luring enraged kings to the great battle stretching from Megiddo to Jerusalem. We also read of seven bowls of God's wrath to be poured out just prior to this ultimate confrontation. Finally, as we will discover, Jesus Himself is seen in unexpected places on earth as He makes His way to the final battle.

In the last chapter, we surveyed the events surrounding the glorious hope of the New Testament: the coming of the Lord, the return of the King. We will now explore the supervening events and epic battle to secure His throne.

The Saints Go Marching On

We know that the antichrist persecutes the saints for a time, but also that his authority is taken away after three and a half years (see Daniel 7:24-27; Revelation 13:5). This three and a half year or *1,260*-day period is completed at the return of Jesus and corresponding resurrection of the saints. The moment Jesus appears, the saints are glorified and thus delivered from persecution. However, Daniel 12:11 tells us there is a total of *1,290* days from the abomination of desolation until the antichrist's end. What happens during this interim of thirty days? Where are Jesus and His army of newly resurrected saints during this period?

It appears that Jesus and His saints are on the earth during this time. In several passages we see glimpses of Him, apparently on His way to the battle of Armageddon. Jesus is marching with His saints (see Habakkuk 3:12-16; Zechariah 14:2-5; Jude 14-15; Psalm 149:5-9), a glorious spectacle to all the earth. Psalm 110 portrays Him with His mighty army executing judgment "among the nations" and "over the wide earth."

In other passages, we see Jesus advancing through places such as Egypt, Edom (modern-day Jordan), Tyre and Sidon (Lebanon), Hamath (Lebanon and Syria), and Assyria (Iraq and Southern Turkey) on His way to Jerusalem (see Joel 3:1-16; Isaiah 11:10-12; 19:18-22; 34:6; 63:1-6; Zechariah 12:1-13:1). All of these places surround Israel and have at times been in conflict with the nation. Joel 3:1-16, Ezekiel 39:25-29, Psalm 102:15-20, Isaiah 42:5-13, and 49:8-26 each show Jesus devastating antichrist strongholds and setting captives free, while Isaiah 63:1 portrays Him in Edom, covered in the blood of His enemies. Just as Hitler filled prison camps with those he considered enemies, it is likely that the antichrist will imprison millions of people (including many Jews and Christians) who refuse to submit to him. There will be a literal fulfillment of Isaiah 42:7, Joel 3:1, and similar passages: Jesus will set the captives free all along His journey through the Middle East, towards the final battle.

The Judgments of God

Following the chronology of the Book of Revelation, the bowls of wrath begin to be poured out directly after the seventh trumpet (and corresponding return of Jesus). It appears that the seven bowls of wrath will be poured out in judgment at the very time Jesus and His saints are marching through the Middle East. This will be a spectacular period of time, unlike any in history, as God gives mankind one final opportunity to repent. As we saw in chapter four, "The Coming of the King," one of God's primary purposes in end-time judgment is bringing the nations to repentance (see Revelation 9:20, 21; 16:9, 11).

Some of the seal judgments could take months or perhaps even a year to unfold (such as the outbreak of world war in the second seal, global famine in the third, and worldwide pestilence in the fourth). Many of the trumpet judgments, however, could be fulfilled in a shorter span of time. It seems that the most protracted of the trumpet judgments takes five months to unfold (see Revelation 9:5), whereas others may only take a few days. The bowl judgments, which begin directly after the seventh trumpet, are each events that could take place very quickly. The entire series of seven bowl judgments could easily happen in the aforementioned thirty-day period of time.

Revelation 19:11-21 and Zechariah 12 and 14 show us the ultimate victory of Jesus once He reaches Jerusalem. The rebellious kings and armies of many nations square off against the Lord and His saints in a battle which stretches from around

Megiddo to somewhere south of Jerusalem. John tells us that the battle stretches for at least 200 miles (*1600 furlongs* in Revelation 14:20). The symbolic language of Scripture describes the battlefield as a winepress and Jesus as the treader of grapes. The kings and armies who come against Him will be crushed in **"the winepress of the fierceness and wrath of Almighty God" (see Revelation 14:19; 19:15).**

The Battle for Jerusalem

Zechariah amplifies the battle for Jerusalem, giving us great detail. All the nations of the earth will gather to fight for control of this city (see Zechariah 12:3). Jesus is destined to reign from Jerusalem (see Zechariah 14:16-17; Luke 1:32; Isaiah 2:3; Micah 4:2) and the antichrist is determined to usurp Jesus' throne there. Satan has set his sights on Jerusalem because the world will be ruled from Mount Zion.

As the epic battle for Jerusalem unfolds, we discover the perilous plight of Israel's inhabitants. Vicious armies siege the city and her defenses fail in several places. Ultimately, half of the inhabitants are conquered and go into captivity (see Zechariah 14:2). The remaining half is hanging on by a thread—until Jesus and His army reach Jerusalem.

When Jesus enters the battle with His glorified army, spectacular events ensue. He splits the Mount of Olives in half, making a way for many Jews to escape the battle (see Zechariah 14:3-5). The presence of Jesus has a powerful effect on every person engaged in the battle. The Jews gain supernatural strength—some become as mighty as David and others as mighty as the angel of God (see Zechariah 12:8). His presence has a potent effect on the vicious armies as well. The attackers on horseback go mad, along with their animals, causing many to be trampled (see Zechariah 12:4). Their flesh, eyes, and tongues begin to melt as though a nuclear bomb has exploded (see Zechariah 14:12). Jesus and His army of saints utterly destroy the antichrist's forces (see Zechariah 12:9).

As mentioned above, this battle becomes the **"the winepress of the fierceness and wrath of Almighty God" (see Revelation 19:15)**. The slaughter of the evil army is so great that blood reaches the horse's bridle in some places. Just as Joshua routed the Amorite armies and then turned to exact vengeance on the five kings (see Joshua 11:16-28), Jesus now moves to finish off the leadership of this satanic force. The antichrist (the beast) and the false prophet **"are cast alive into the lake of fire burning with brimstone" (see Revelation 19:20)**. **"The dragon, that serpent of old, who is the Devil and Satan" (see Revelation 20:2-3)** is bound for a thousand years and cast into the bottomless pit. Jesus stands triumphant over the battlefield, having destroyed all who opposed Him.

The Manifestation of Messiah

In the concluding moments of the battle, thousands of years of prophetic promises have come to a head. Jesus, having triumphed over the powers of evil, stands in the hush of victory as the conquering King. Millions of Jews who have fought alongside Jesus and His army are faced with a catastrophic question and its undeniable answer, "Who is this Captain of the Hosts, this Conquering King? He is Jesus of Nazareth! The One we have reviled and rejected for two thousand years is our long-awaited Messiah!"

Jesus describes the moment Israel sees Him for who He really is:

> "And I will pour out on the house of David and
> the inhabitants of Jerusalem a spirit of grace and
> pleas for mercy, so that, when they look on me,
> on him whom they have pierced, they shall mourn
> for him, as one mourns for an only child, and weep
> bitterly over him, as one weeps over a firstborn.
>
> "On that day the mourning in Jerusalem will
> be as great as the mourning for Hadad-rimmon in
> the plain of Megiddo.
>
> "On that day there shall be a fountain opened
> for the house of David and the inhabitants of
> Jerusalem, to cleanse them from sin and unclean-
> ness" (Zechariah 12:10-11, 13:1 ESV).

Israel will look upon the One they pierced at Calvary. They
will see the Son of God for who He really is, and they will
weep for Him as one weeps for an only son. At this moment,
every Jew who sees Him will believe in Him. They will realize
that the Lamb who was slain and the Lion of Judah are one
and the same person. He was their Suffering Servant and He is
their Conquering King. The One who bled on the cross at their
hands is now covered in the blood of their enemies, having defeated many armies on their behalf. In that day, Romans 11:26
will be fulfilled, **"All Israel will be saved."** Or, as Zechariah
puts it, **"In that day a fountain shall be opened for the
house of David and for the inhabitants of Jerusalem, for
sin and for uncleanness" (Zechariah 13:1).** Their sins will be
washed away because they will accept Jesus as their Savior when
they see Him at the end of this battle.

The Sheep and Goat Judgment

Life on earth will never be same after the battle of
Armageddon. As discussed above, Satan, the antichrist, and the

false prophet are defeated and cast into the lake of fire or the bottomless pit, respectively. All resistance to Jesus has been dealt with and thus He is the ultimate authority. Matthew 25:31-46 reveals many details about the time following the battle. Jesus will sit as the King and Judge over humanity. He will gather the nations before Him and will separate people and nations into two distinct groups: sheep and goats.

There are three categories of people at the time of this judgment: saints in glorified bodies, Jews who have just accepted Jesus as Messiah, and others **"who** [are] **left of all the nations which came against Jerusalem" (see Zechariah 14:16).** Saints in glorified bodies have obviously already been counted as "sheep" since they have already trusted in Jesus, the Shepherd. It seems that the newly converted Jews will also be judged as sheep because, to use the language of Romans 11:6, **"all Israel"** has just been saved.

However, "those who are left" of the nations, who were not killed in the battle, anticipate a time of judgment. They will each stand before Jesus, and He will judge them based on how they treated His brothers, Jews and Christians (see Matthew 25:39). If they fed His brothers, gave them shelter and clothing, and visited them in prison, Jesus would count them as sheep and they will be permitted to enter into His kingdom on earth in the millennium. If they did not care for His brothers in this way, they would be deemed "goats" and perish in eternal fire (see Matthew 25:41). This passage seems to imply that Jesus, in the sheep and goat judgment, will evaluate how everyone treated His people during the intense times of persecution under the antichrist.

It is likely that entire nations will be counted as "sheep nations" in this epoch of judgment. According to Matthew 25:32, Jesus will gather the "nations" before His throne and He will separate people "one from another" as sheep or goats. This may imply that the individual leaders of some nations made godly decisions to govern their nations in a way that God counts as righteous. Therefore, there may be nations that exist today which are permitted to continue into the millennium. Imagine that Germany, the United States, Brazil, or Japan may continue as a nation in the age to come. This revelation should serve as a great motivator to governmental leaders and intercessors in the present age.

It is possible this period of judgment lasts for forty-five days. It will take some time for the multitudes "left of all the nations" in the four corners of the earth to come before Jesus. As previously discussed, one thousand two hundred and sixty days from the abomination of desolation until the second coming plus an additional thirty days in which Jesus and His army march through the Middle East would complete the one thousand two hundred and ninety day period of Daniel 12:11. The additional forty-five days of the sheep and goat judgment complete the one thousand three hundred and thirty-five day period mentioned in Daniel 12:12, **"Blessed is he who waits, and comes to the one thousand three hundred and thirty-five days,"** as they will enter the age of the kingdom of God on earth. Daniel himself will enter into his inheritance at the end of the one thousand three hundred and thirty-five days, ruling and reigning with Jesus (see Daniel 12:13).

The End of the Beginning

The transition between the battle in Revelation 19 and the beginning of the millennium in Revelation 20 is the great hinge of eternity. Jesus will conquer the evil armies and capture Jerusalem because Jerusalem is the city of His throne (see Isaiah 2:3; Luke 1:32-33). After judging the nations, He will appoint His government and inaugurate His one thousand year reign with the saints. He will reign as King from Jerusalem, restoring the planet and preparing the way for the coming of the Father (see Revelation 21:1-7). He will make way for heaven and earth to become one (see Ephesians 1:10).

More than six thousand years of human history culminate with the victory of the Last Adam and defeat of Satan, the serpent from the garden. The great battle and ensuing sheep and goat judgment are not the end; they are merely the end of the beginning. From this point forward a new era begins: the kingdom of God on earth.

Thanks to God for the hope of Scripture, the King is coming and He will make all things right and all things new!

CHAPTER 6

THE COMING OF THE KINGDOM

The Kingdom Comes at Last

Following the sheep and goat judgment of Matthew 25, Jesus begins His reign as King. We discover many fascinating features of this unique time in redemptive history. We know from Psalm 72:8 that, **"He shall have dominion also from sea to sea, and from the River to the ends of the earth."** Zechariah 14:9 declares **"The Lord shall be King over all the earth."** Jeremiah 3:17 prophesies, **"At that time Jerusalem shall be called The Throne of the LORD, and all the nations shall be gathered to it."**

In chapter 5 we contemplated the great conflict and consequent victory of King Jesus as He assumed authority over the earth. Let us now behold the dream of God and the destiny of humanity: the inauguration of the kingdom of God on the earth.

Jesus will sit on His throne in Jerusalem. He will rule the earth from Mount Zion. He will judge nations and disciple kings as they come to submit themselves to Him. Consider Isaiah's vision of Jesus' future administration:

The word that Isaiah the son of Amoz saw concerning Judah and Jerusalem.

Now it shall come to pass in the latter days that the mountain of the LORD's house shall be established on the top of the mountains, and shall be exalted above the hills; and all nations shall flow to it.

Many people shall come and say, "Come, and let us go up to the mountain of the LORD, to the house of the God of Jacob; He will teach us His ways, and we shall walk in His paths." For out of Zion shall go forth the law, and the word of the LORD from Jerusalem.

He shall judge between the nations, and rebuke many people; they shall beat their swords into plowshares, and their spears into pruning hooks; nation shall not lift up sword against nation, neither shall they learn war anymore (Isaiah 2:1-4).

This time will be like no other time in history. Jesus will be physically present as the glorified King of the earth. He will rule in partnership with a government of resurrected saints, over a thriving planet of people who have the choice to accept Him or reject Him. During this future age, the earth will be restored to the paradise it was originally created to be. This reign of Jesus and His saints will be an eternal testimony to powers and principalities that He is ultimately wise and righteous, the perfect King (see Ephesians 3:10).

Jesus, King of the Earth!

Revelation 20 gives us an overview of the main features of the first thousand years of the kingdom age:

> Then I saw an angel coming down from heaven, having the key to the bottomless pit and a great chain in his hand.
>
> He laid hold of the dragon, that serpent of old, who is the Devil and Satan, and bound him for a thousand years;
>
> and he cast him into the bottomless pit, and shut him up, and set a seal on him, so that he should deceive the nations no more till the thousand years were finished. But after these things he must be released for a little while.
>
> And I saw thrones, and they sat on them, and judgment was committed to them. Then I saw the souls of those who had been beheaded for their witness to Jesus and for the word of God, who had not worshiped the beast or his image, and had not received his mark on their foreheads or on their hands. And they lived and reigned with Christ for a thousand years.
>
> But the rest of the dead did not live again until the thousand years were finished. This is the first resurrection.
>
> Blessed and holy is he who has part in the first resurrection. Over such the second death has no power, but they shall be priests of God and of Christ, and shall reign with Him a thousand years (Revelation 20:1-6).

The "first resurrection" takes place at the second coming of Jesus. When He returns, every believer from all time will be caught up and given a resurrected body (see I Thessalonians 4:13-17; I Corinthians 15:51-55). These saints in glorified bodies **"shall be priests of God and of Christ, and shall reign with Him a thousand years" (see Revelation 20:6).** This speaks of their millennial role in ministry (priests) and government (reign with Him). It has been suggested that the wedding supper of the Lamb (see Revelation 19:9) takes place at the beginning of this one thousand years (also called "the millennium"), or even at the end of it. However, another possibility is that the entire one thousand years is a celebration of Jesus' marriage to His bride.

During the millennium, Jesus and His saints will oversee an operation to restore creation, rebuild ruined cities, and reverse the effects of the Adamic curse (see Revelation 20:1-4; Isaiah 49:8, 61:4; Ezekiel 36:33-36). Further, during the millennium a special seat of authority is granted to end-time martyrs (see Revelation 20:4).

In chapter 4, "The Coming of the King," we looked at Daniel's vision of the Father giving Jesus authority over the earth (see Daniel 7:9-14. This is the heavenly "coronation" of Christ, just before He steps into the earth realm to conquer His enemies and begin His reign. The vision continues to unveil glorious realities through the end of the chapter. In Daniel 7:15-28, we witness the evil of the antichrist (the little horn of 7:8) and his federation of ten nations. We watch as they are defeated and the antichrist is thrown into the lake of fire (compare with Revelation 19:20). Finally, we read **"Then the kingdom and dominion, and the greatness of the kingdoms under the whole heaven, shall be given to the people, the saints of the Most High. His kingdom is an everlasting kingdom, and all dominions shall serve and obey Him" (Daniel 7:27).** King Jesus has chosen to share His reign with a queen: His people and His bride (see Hebrews 2:5-8).

The millennium will be the first time in history when God will be King on earth and all the nations will be subject to Him. As we will see in the next chapter, glorified saints will not be the only inhabitants of the earth during this time. The planet will also be populated with millions of humans in natural bodies who will continue to have freewill, reproduce, and even potentially die (see Zechariah 14:16-19; Isaiah 65:20).

Ruling and Reigning with Jesus

Our daily lives are vitally connected to the future coming of the kingdom of God. Jesus taught us a radical way of life in Matthew 5-7, the "Sermon on the Mount." He presents a way of living that is contrary to fallen human nature, but is a reflection of His nature and His kingdom: choosing to be poor in spirit, living in meekness, giving our possessions away to others, blessing our enemies rather than retaliating, and concealing the good things we do so that we receive no recognition from men. When we live this way, we reflect the age to come into our present age; we become a testimony to the earth and manifest His future kingdom in the present day.

Gregory Beale, professor of New Testament at Westminster Theological Seminary, teaches in his "Biblical Theology" course that "understanding eschatology is the key to sanctification in the Christian life." In other words, the more we understand the link between our daily walk and our station in the age to come, the more we will seek the grace of God for personal transformation. Living the "Sermon on the Mount" lifestyle is difficult and completely "counter" to the culture of the world. However, this lifestyle fits us to reign with Jesus and positions us to receive great promises (see II Timothy 2:12). These promises have implications for our lives now, but they will be fully manifest when the kingdom of God comes to earth: we will see God, possess the kingdom, inherit the earth, and receive great eternal rewards (see Matthew 5:3-12).

When Jesus returns to earth, every believer will receive a glorified (or *glory-fied*) body—just as Jesus did after His resurrection (see Philippians 3:20-21). This means that the glory of God will transform our natural body into something super-natural—our mortality will put on immortality (see I Corinthians 15:53). In this resurrection, we will differ from one another in our degree of glory (see I Corinthians 15:41-42), magnitude of reward (see Luke 19:11-27; I Corinthians 3:11-15), and level of responsibility (see Matthew 25:14-30). Those who are faithful in this life may be given cities or entire nations to rule over in the age to come. Others may be given responsibility for far less, perhaps they will be given charge of a neighborhood or a public park. It seems that many who are unfaithful with what they are given in this life will lose the opportunity for government and will be in the station of a servant in the millennium (see I Corinthians 3:10-15). Many who insist on being the exalted in this life will be the least of all in the kingdom to come (see Matthew 23:10-12).

The New Testament reveals that our present character and stewardship will establish our eternal station. Paul rebukes the litigious church at Corinth while lamenting their elders' failure to administer justice. If we will one day judge the world and even angels, we must exercise godly judgment in this life. **"Do you not know that the saints will judge the world? And if the world will be judged by you, are you unworthy to judge the smallest matters? Do you not know that we shall judge angels? How much more, things that pertain to this life?" (I Corinthians 6:2-3)**

When Jesus presides over the nations as King and Judge, He will entrust great responsibility only to those who were faithful in earthly matters. Consider the parable of the minas:

> **Therefore He said: "A certain nobleman went into a far country to receive for himself a kingdom and to return.**

"So he called ten of his servants, delivered to them ten minas, and said to them, 'Do business till I come.'

"But his citizens hated him, and sent a delegation after him, saying, 'We will not have this man to reign over us.'

"And so it was that when he returned, having received the kingdom, he then commanded these servants, to whom he had given the money, to be called to him, that he might know how much every man had gained by trading.

"Then came the first, saying, 'Master, your mina has earned ten minas.'

"And he said to him, 'Well done, good servant; because you were faithful in a very little, have authority over ten cities.'

"And the second came, saying, 'Master, your mina has earned five minas.'

"Likewise he said to him, 'You also be over five cities.'

"Then another came, saying, 'Master, here is your mina, which I have kept put away in a handkerchief.

'For I feared you, because you are an austere man. You collect what you did not deposit, and reap what you did not sow.'

"And he said to him, 'Out of your own mouth I will judge you, you wicked servant. You knew that I was an austere man, collecting what I did not deposit and reaping what I did not sow.

'Why then did you not put my money in the bank, that at my coming I might have collected it with interest?'

"And he said to those who stood by, 'Take the mina from him, and give it to him who has ten minas.'

(But they said to him, 'Master, he has ten minas.')

'For I say to you, that to everyone who has will be given; and from him who does not have, even what he has will be taken away from him.

'But bring here those enemies of mine, who did not want me to reign over them, and slay them before me'" (Luke 19:12–27 NKJV).

The nobleman in this parable is Jesus. He entrusted his treasure to stewards before going away to receive a kingdom. Likewise, Jesus has entrusted His people with a sacred vocation to steward our gifts and callings while we await His return. He has ascended to heaven and is awaiting the time the Father will send Him back to reign over the kingdom of God on earth. Many will be counted faithful and called "good servants" when He returns, having invested their "minas" to increase His kingdom. Others will be deemed "wicked servants" because they squandered the treasure He entrusted to them. Those who are faithful will be given much to govern in the age to come, even the oversight of five or ten cities. Those who are unfaithful stewards will lose their reward or even receive judgment.

This parable is encouraging in light of the value of a mina—approximately sixty days wages. Therefore, the servant who was given ten cities to reign over obtained this inheritance for stewarding a relatively small trust of two month's wages. We are not required to be great, wealthy, or powerful in this life in order to be a king in the age to come. We need only to be faithful. Indeed, those who are faithful with the "little" they have been given will be entrusted with "much" in the coming kingdom (see Matthew 25:23).

Greatness in eternity will not correlate to our greatness in this life, but to our faithfulness! May we be faithful in the small and great things the Lord entrusts to us.

CHAPTER 7

THE NATIONS AND ISRAEL IN THE AGE TO COME

Kingdom Classes

In chapter 6, we examined the role the saints will play in the millennial kingdom. What about the others who pass through the sheep and goat judgment into the kingdom—those who were not already believers at the second coming of Jesus?

It is evident from many passages in Scripture that the saints in glorified bodies are not the only people living in the millennium. We know that believers are made perfect and incorruptible once they are glorified at the coming of the Lord (see Hebrews 12:23, 11:40; I Corinthians 15:49; 15:54). However, it is clear that there are some imperfect people living on earth during the time when Jesus is reigning in Jerusalem. Some apparently refuse to obey God's command to worship at the annual Feast of Tabernacles (see Zechariah 14:16-19), or refuse to participate in God's millennial rebuilding effort (see Isaiah 60:10-12). Resurrected saints will reign over a planet full of people in natural bodies who have not yet been perfected and who may rebel against Jesus.

It is also evident that there are two classes of these people in natural bodies: Gentiles and newly converted Jews (see Zechariah 8:20-23; Isaiah 61:4-11). The Gentiles are those "left of all the nations which came against Jerusalem" that we discussed in chapter 5. The newly converted Jews appear to play an important role in the millennium. They will become the nation of priests that God originally intended them to be (see Exodus 19:6). At Mount Sinai, God first invited Israel to be His people and His representatives—a kingdom of priests and a holy nation. Israel refused God at Sinai, sending Moses to Him instead of going themselves (see Exodus 20:19). This repudiation dramatically altered God's strategy for them. However, the Lord has not forgotten His original intention for His people Israel. In the age to come, resurrected saints will be God's government, and Israel will be His priesthood.

> **"Yes, many peoples and strong nations shall come to seek the LORD of hosts in Jerusalem, and to pray before the LORD."**
>
> **"Thus says the LORD of hosts: 'In those days ten men from every language of the nations shall grasp the sleeve of a Jewish man, saying, "Let us go with you, for we have heard that God is with you"'"** (Zechariah 8:22-23).

Since the time Zechariah prophesied these things, nothing remotely similar has happened in Israel; the prophecy is hitherto unfulfilled. This passage pictures people from many nations coming to Jerusalem to seek Jesus, who will physically reside there. They will pray before Him and He will personally teach and judge between them (see Micah 4:1-3). Further, people from every ethnic group will latch on to the Jewish people, asking them about God. Zechariah's prophecy is clear: Millions of Jews who accept Jesus at the time of His second coming (see

Zechariah 12:10, 13:1) will be His "nation of priests" in the age to come (see Isaiah 56:6-8, 61:6-9). They, along with the saints, will disciple the Gentiles from many nations. The will be known among the nations as "the holy people, the redeemed of the Lord" and they will be "sought out" by all (see Isaiah 62:11-12).

In the present age, things are virtually opposite from God's ultimate intent. Unregenerate Gentiles seem to hold far more positions in government than God's saints. Further, rather than discipling nations, Israel is ordained to be made "jealous" and evangelized by the predominately Gentile church (see Romans 11:7-15). The church is God's current kingdom of priests and holy nation (see I Peter 2:9)—but Israel is ultimately destined to join her.

The Millennial Occupation: Restoring the Earth

There are unique features of the millennium, which distinguish it from this present age and eternity, the age to come. For example, in Isaiah 65:20-25 God speaks of a time on earth when babies will continue to be born, yet much like before the flood of Genesis 7, a typical lifespan will be hundreds of years, **"as the days of a tree" (see Isaiah 65:22).** During this time, if someone dies at one hundred years old, we will assume they must have been a sinner because they were not permitted to live out their full years. A person of one hundred years old will be considered to be a child. This scenario does not fit in this age (because one hundred years is a long time to live) or in the eternal age to come (because no one will die in the eternal age (see Revelation 21:4; I Corinthians 15:26).

The millennium seems to be an intermediate epoch before the eternal age begins. According to Isaiah 65, during this intermediate era there will be no more treachery, enmity between animals, or violence—even lions "will eat straw like an ox." The earth will be like the Garden of Eden again, full of peace and the presence of God. Consider another prophecy of Isaiah:

> **"The wolf also shall dwell with the lamb, the leopard shall lie down with the young goat, the calf and the young lion and the fatling together; and a little child shall lead them.**
>
> **"The cow and the bear shall graze; their young ones shall lie down together; and the lion shall eat straw like the ox.**
>
> **"The nursing child shall play by the cobra's hole, and the weaned child shall put his hand in the viper's den.**
>
> **"They shall not hurt nor destroy in all My holy mountain, for the earth shall be full of the knowledge of the LORD As the waters cover the sea.**
>
> **"For the Gentiles shall seek Him, and His resting place shall be glorious" (see Isaiah 11:6-10).**

Here we see a beautiful picture of creation restored to pre-fall condition. Everyone will intimately know the Lord and will be at peace with one another. The earth will be His resting place and it will be glorious. We know that cities and nations will be in need of comprehensive restoration after the massive destruction in the Book of Revelation. Below we will see several prophetic scenes of this great rebuilding that restores the planet during the one thousand years.

Jesus was individually anointed by the Holy Spirit to fulfill Isaiah 61:1-3 during His earthly ministry. He preached the gospel to the poor, healed the brokenhearted, proclaimed liberty to the captives, proclaimed both the favor and the vengeance of God, and He comforted Zion offering them beauty for ashes, joy for mourning, and a spirit of praise for heaviness.

Likewise, the Spirit corporately anoints the church in this age to fulfill Isaiah 61:1-11, albeit spiritually rather than physically. We set captives free from the devil but not necessarily from prisons. We restore ruined lives but not necessarily ruined cities. However, in the millennium, Isaiah 61:1-11 will be literally and physically fulfilled as the saints and Israel minister to the Gentiles and lead them in a great project to restore the earth after the devastations of the great tribulation. Read the passage below with this perspective:

> They shall build up the ancient ruins; they shall raise up the former devastations; they shall repair the ruined cities, the devastations of many generations.
>
> Strangers shall stand and tend your flocks; foreigners shall be your plowmen and vinedressers;
>
> but you shall be called the priests of the LORD; they shall speak of you as the ministers of our God; you shall eat the wealth of the nations, and in their glory you shall boast.
>
> Instead of your shame there shall be a double portion; instead of dishonor they shall rejoice in their lot; therefore in their land they shall possess a double portion; they shall have everlasting joy.
>
> Their offspring shall be known among the nations, and their descendants in the midst of the peoples; all who see them shall acknowledge them, that they are an offspring the LORD has blessed.
>
> So the Lord GOD will cause righteousness and praise to spring forth before all the nations (see Isaiah 61:4-7, 9, 11 ESV).

Israel, a nation of priests, will step into the fullness of their calling in the millennium. They will teach the Gentiles and will be called **"priests of the Lord"** and **"the ministers of our God."** Israel (and the saints) will be **"known among the**

nations" as **"an offspring the Lord has blessed."** Many of Israel will be in positions of spiritual leadership, as many glorified saints will be in positions of governmental leadership and vice versa. Together, all peoples will participate in global restoration as they **"build up the ancient ruins . . . raise up the former devastations . . . repair the ruined cities, the devastations of many generations."**

Many other passages speak of the millennial rebuilding and restoration, such as Amos 9:14 and Isaiah 58:12. Ezekiel vividly describes this unique phase of redemptive history when the earth is restored to the glory of Eden:

> **Thus says the Lord GOD: "On the day that I cleanse you from all your iniquities, I will also enable you to dwell in the cities, and the ruins shall be rebuilt.**
>
> **"The desolate land shall be tilled instead of lying desolate in the sight of all who pass by.**
>
> **"So they will say, 'This land that was desolate has become like the garden of Eden; and the wasted, desolate, and ruined cities are now fortified and inhabited.'**
>
> **"Then the nations which are left all around you shall know that I, the LORD, have rebuilt the ruined places and planted what was desolate. I, the LORD, have spoken it, and I will do it" (Ezekiel 36:33-36).**

This restoration of cities and nations is more than a mere rebuilding—it is a supernaturally redemptive restoration. It is not only that structures will be rebuilt—the effects of the curse will be fully rolled back (see Isaiah 11:6-10). Jesus is currently leading His church in the restoration of the souls of men. During the millennium, He will lead His people in the restoration of the whole earth.

The War to End All Wars

As we have seen, the millennial kingdom will be remarkable—like no other time in history. The culmination of the millennium will be the most remarkable of all. At the end of one thousand years of restoration and perfect Divine government, God does something shocking, even puzzling. He releases Satan from captivity to **"go out and deceive the nations" (see Revelation 20:7-8).**

Why would the omnipotent, omniscient God allow Satan to be released after being bound for one thousand years? One of the primary reasons the millennium has been a glorious time of restoration and peace is because Satan has been imprisoned. However, God determines that the paramount phase of redemptive history involves the liberation of the devil. Could this possibly be a good idea?

The wisdom of the Almighty in this decision is stunning. There will be billions of offspring born to the Gentiles and Jews during the thousand-year reign of Jesus. They have grown up in an almost Garden-of-Eden-like existence. They have lived under the glorious government of Jesus and His resurrected saints, while hearing the truth proclaimed with unparalleled clarity and anointing. They have never encountered the challenge of resisting demonic temptation to sin—which has been the relentless ordeal of everyone alive from Eden to Armageddon. They are like a planet of Adams and Eves prior the serpent's suggestion to eat the forbidden fruit. They have never *fully* had the opportunity to choose God over sin.

God wants a people who choose to love Him. He could have made us like robots who have no choice but to say "yes," but instead He desires those who desire Him. Just as every person in this age is tested to see whether we will chose Him over sin and self, the release of Satan will provide a "Garden of Eden test" for the "millennials"—the generations born during the thousand years. They will be tempted to follow a different king and they must choose to remain loyal to Jesus:

> **Now when the thousand years have expired, Satan will be released from his prison and will go out to deceive the nations which are in the four corners of the earth, Gog and Magog, to gather them together to battle, whose number is as the sand of the sea (Revelation 20:7-8).**

The Shortest Battle of All Time

Amazingly, multitudes of people in the millennial Eden choose to follow the serpent. It appears that billions reject the Lordship of Jesus and choose to follow Satan. We are not told what form the devil takes when he goes out to deceive the nations. He may appear as a beautiful and powerful king, who is challenging Jesus's throne. He may speak to the people's inward frustrations and offer them an alternative lifestyle: "Why do you always have to follow His rules? Why not live a little? Be free?" Whatever strategy he employs, it is very effective because the army he raises to fight Jesus is as numerous "as the sand of the sea."

It may take weeks or even months for him to gather this mob—we do not know how long. We only know how long it takes for Jesus to win the battle when Satan marches on Jerusalem. It is the shortest battle of all time:

> **They went up on the breadth of the earth and surrounded the camp of the saints and the beloved city. And fire came down from God out of heaven and devoured them.**

The devil, who deceived them, was cast into the lake of fire and brimstone where the beast and the false prophet are. And they will be tormented day and night forever and ever (Revelation 20:9-10).

It is as though God looks down on the gathering battle, which is reminiscent of the battle for Jerusalem we see in Revelation 19 and Zechariah 12 and 14. The Father remembers the trauma of that battle and says, "We're not doing this again." With one wave of His hand, fire is released from heaven to burn up the billions who planned to attack Jesus. Satan is then captured again and thrown into the lake of fire to be tormented forever.

This is truly the "last battle"—never again will there be war. The millennium will be preparation for eternity and in it, many prophecies will be fulfilled in measure. However, as creation enters the next phase of existence—*eternity*—many prophecies will be ultimately fulfilled:

They shall beat their swords into plowshares, and their spears into pruning hooks; nation shall not lift up sword against nation, neither shall they learn war anymore.

But everyone shall sit under his vine and under his fig tree, and no one shall make them afraid; for the mouth of the LORD of hosts has spoken (see Micah 4:3-4).

Only those faithful to Jesus are left after the last battle of Revelation 20. They are ready to enter eternity, the final phase of redemptive history. God the Father will be on earth, heaven and earth will be one, and the universe will be our domain.

The Apostle Paul erupted with worship and adoration to the Lord as he marveled at His plan to sovereignly save Gentile and Jew (see Romans 11:33-36). So let us marvel and explode with praise as we ponder the plan of God outlined above! In the end, not one of those that the Father gave Jesus will be missing (see John 6:39). Jew and Gentile, sinner and saint—Jesus will give God the Father glory for each one in the age to come. He will never demand devotion, yet in that day He will be adored from **"sea to sea, and from the River to the ends of the earth" (see Psalm 72:8).**

For of Him and through Him and to Him are all things, to whom be glory forever. Amen (Romans 11:36).

CHAPTER 8

THE NEW BEGINNING AND NEW CREATION

The Great White Throne Judgment

Following the battle for Jerusalem in Revelation 19, Jesus presides over the sheep and goat judgment, which we examined previously. It appears that after the last battle of Revelation 20, Jesus presides over the great white throne judgment of those who have rejected Christ from every generation (see Revelation 20:11-15). Their names are not written in the book of life, so they are eternally condemned to the lake of fire, which is called the "second death" (see Revelation 21:8). The resurrection for the great white throne judgment is the second resurrection, as contrasted with the "first resurrection" of Revelation 20:5, I Corinthians 15:20-55, I and Thessalonians 4:14-17.

The language describing the judgment awaiting those who reject Christ is quite graphic. In Revelation 21:8, we read of **"the cowardly, unbelieving, abominable, murderers, sexually immoral, sorcerers, idolaters, and all liars** [who] **shall have their part in the lake which burns with fire and brimstone, which is the second death."** Revelation 14:10-11 tells us these will **"drink of the wine of the wrath of God, which is poured out full strength into the cup of**

His indignation. [They] shall be tormented with fire and brimstone in the presence of the holy angels and in the presence of the Lamb. And the smoke of their torment ascends forever and ever; and they have no rest day or night."

This topic of eternal judgment in the lake of fire is distinctly eschatological. Jesus is returning not only as the heavenly Bridegroom and King, but also as the *Judge*. The second coming of Christ and establishment of His kingdom will display all three of these identities. The New Testament often speaks of Jesus as the Judge of the world (see John 5:22, Acts 17:31). Jesus Himself teaches us more about the horrors of judgment in hell than anyone else in the Bible. He spoke of the destruction awaiting those who walk the broad path (see Matthew 7:14) and of the furnace of fire and the wailing and gnashing of teeth that awaits those who practice lawlessness (see Matthew 13:41-42). He also said those who are "sentenced" to hell are eternally tormented by worms and unquenchable fire (see Matthew 23:33; Mark 9:43-49). Judgment in the lake of fire is a weighty end-time theme that we must not fail to consider.

Thank You Jesus for saving us from **"the wrath to come" (see I Thessalonians 1:10)!**

Preparing the Way for the Father

In the last chapter we read of the supernatural restoration accomplished during the thousand-year reign of Christ. The judgment of Revelation 20:11-15 is the final phase of this restoration. There remains an ultimate mysterious purpose of this thousand-year restoration: to prepare the way for the Father to come to earth.

As David Sliker teaches in *End Times Simplified:*

> *The main goal of Jesus' thousand year reign will be to prepare the nations for the coming of His Father to earth. God has longed since the Fall to be fully with us again and Jesus has always been committed to making this a reality. He will labor with the saints to prepare every nation and people . . .* (page 135).

John the Baptist "prepared the way for the Lord" before Jesus' *first* coming (see Mark 1:3), and the body of Christ is now preparing the way for His *second* coming. The inhabitants of millennial earth will prepare the way for the Father to come and dwell with them. God and man, heaven and earth, Jerusalem and New Jerusalem, will come together as one:

> **Now I saw a new heaven and a new earth, for the first heaven and the first earth had passed away. Also there was no more sea.**
>
> **Then I, John, saw the holy city, New Jerusalem, coming down out of heaven from God, prepared as a bride adorned for her husband.**
>
> **And I heard a loud voice from heaven saying, "Behold, the tabernacle of God is with men, and He will dwell with them, and they shall be His people . . . " (see Revelation 21:1-3).**

The final epoch of redemptive history begins with the union of the heavenly realm and the earthly realm—the habitation of God and the habitation of mankind become one and God dwells in the midst (see Ephesians 1:9-10).

The Salvation of All of Creation

The New Testament speaks of the revolutionary change that salvation brings to an individual "in Christ." **"Therefore, if anyone is in Christ, he is a new creation; old things have passed away; behold, all things have become new" (II Corinthians 5:17).** All old things pass away and all things become new! We are cleansed of evil, and we receive a new heart and experience a new beginning (see Ezekiel 36:26; Jeremiah 31:31-34). We are made into a suitable dwelling for God, and we are filled with His presence, the Holy Spirit (see I Corinthians 6:9). We will marvel at God's glorious salvation for all of eternity.

Further, the Savior's saving work extends beyond individuals "in Christ." The culmination of His glorious salvation will be a "new creation" in the new heaven and the new earth (see Revelation 21:1). Revelation 21:3-5 closely parallels II Corinthians 5:17, **"God Himself will be with them and be their God . . . The former things have passed away. Then He who sat on the throne said, 'Behold, I make all things new.'"**

All old and evil things will pass away, and God will make all things new. The earth will be a suitable dwelling for the Lord, and He will come and fill it with His presence. Heaven and earth will become one as the universe experiences a new beginning.

Gregory Beale has written extensively on this topic in his tome, *A New Testament Biblical Theology*. He expounds upon many parallels between the work of salvation in the individual and the eschatological theme of the new creation. The new creation work God has done for the individual believer in this age foreshadows what He will do for all of creation in the age to come.

This new creation reality is also at the heart of the "gospel of the kingdom" message. Matthew 24:14 portends this will be preached to all nations before the end of the age: "King Jesus died and was raised—*to save and restore all who call on His name.* He will return to establish His kingdom on earth—*to save and restore all of creation!*"

What We've All Been Waiting For

This "new creation" is what all of creation longs for. Romans 8:18-30 reveals that creation is groaning and travailing with the longing to be delivered from bondage to corruption. This corruption entered in as part of the curse when mankind fell (see Genesis 3:16-19). This groaning for liberty besets the natural order as well as humanity. The soil longs to be freed from the curse of toil, and our neighbors groan to be freed from the curse of sin and sickness—whether they recognize it or not.

The Greek word for "new" heaven and "new" earth in Revelation 21:1 is *kainos.* This is the same Greek word used for born-again believers as new creations in II Corinthians 5:17 and Galatians 6:15. We are the new creation manifested in this age—a foreshadowing and demonstration of the *kainos* reality of the age to come, from now until the fullness comes. We are meant to walk as witnesses to the present age that the temporal world is not all there is. The creation is looking for sons and daughters of God—*kainos* believers, who will be agents for their liberation (see Romans 8:19-21).

At the second coming of Christ, believers will receive that which we have longed for—**"the adoption, the redemption of our body" (see Romans 8:23).** At this time, old things pass away and all things are made new—physically! We get a glorious body, just like Jesus' glorified body (see Philippians 3:21). Likewise, when the fullness of the Godhead comes to dwell on earth (see Revelation 21:1-5), all of creation receives a similar transformation. **"The first heaven and the first earth pass away"** and **"a new heaven and a new earth"** come forth **(see Revelation 21:1).** Believers are destined to receive a body with the supernatural nature of Jesus' body *and* creation is destined to receive a supernatural nature like heaven's.

The Restoration of All Things

God has declared His purpose in redemptive history. His ultimate objective is **"the restoration of all things" (see Acts 3:21).** This restoration will include "all things" affected by the Fall: humanity, the animal kingdom, botanical life, the elements, the weather, and more. God has also **made known to us the mystery of His will, according to His good pleasure which He purposed in Himself, that in the dispensation of the fullness of the times He might gather together in one all things in Christ, both which are in heaven and which are on earth—in Him" (Ephesians 1:9-10).** It is a mystery, but God intends for all things in heaven and earth to become one. The church has been praying for two thousand years that it would be **"on earth as it is in heaven" (see Matthew 6:10),** and this prayer will be answered.

God's redemptive power is seen dramatically in this age when the life of a fallen sinner is redeemed. Our new creation lives to display His glory. In the same way, God's redemptive power will be seen on a global scale when the whole earth receives its new creation, heavenly nature. At that time, **"the earth will be filled with the knowledge of the glory of the Lord" (see Habakkuk 2:14).** John writes of this epic new beginning, **"And God will wipe away every tear from their eyes; there shall be no more death, nor sorrow, nor crying. There shall be no more pain . . . And He said to me, 'Write, for these words are true and faithful.' And He said to me, 'It is done!'" (Revelation 21:4-6)**

The Father declares, **"It is done!"** at the consummation of His global redemption, just as Jesus declared, **"It is finished!" (see John 19:30)** when He completed His work on the cross. Jesus' work restored mankind to the glory Adam forfeited, and the Father will restore heaven and earth to the glory of Eden.

The Old Testament tabernacle in the wilderness foreshadowed God's eternal residence with man. The cloud by day and fire by night manifested His presence to Israel. When God makes His home on the earth, such will be the manifestation of His glory that there will be **"no need of the sun or of the moon to shine in it, for the glory of God illuminated it" (see Revelation 21:23).** His splendor and majesty will light up the universe. There will also be **"no temple in it, for the Lord God Almighty and the Lamb are its temple" (see Revelation 21:22).** His manifest presence will fill the cosmos.

The Eternal City

The attributes of the eternal city in Revelation 21:10-27 bring to mind the many throne room scenes throughout Scripture. Compare the splendorous walls, foundation stones, and streets of the city with the imagery in Revelation 4:3-6, Exodus 24:9-11, and Ezekiel 1:22-28. The entire city is God's throne room! Revelation 21:16 tells us the **"length, width, breadth** [of the city] **are equal"**—this is the same language used to describe the Holy of Holies in Solomon's temple (see I Kings 6:20). As the cross of Christ gave access to the throne of God by a **"new and living way" (see Hebrews 10:19-22, 4:16),** "the restoration of all things" enables God's servants to dwell in the "throne city" with Him. **"The throne of God and of the Lamb shall be in it, and His servants shall serve Him. They shall see His face, and His name shall be on their foreheads" (Revelation 22:3-4).**

In *The City of God and the Goal of Creation*, T. Desmond Alexander posits that God's transcendent purpose for mankind is the co-habitation of God and man. His purpose in the Garden of Eden, the tabernacle, the temple, the incarnation, and the outpouring of the Holy Spirit has been towards that end. Only in the throne city of the New Jerusalem, however, will this dream of God's heart be fully realized. Alexander summarizes, "At the very heart of God's plan for the world stands an extraordinary city. Beginning with the Garden of Eden in Genesis and ending with the New Jerusalem in Revelation, the biblical story reveals how God has been working throughout history to establish a city filled with His glorious presence."

What are the implications of such a strategy in the heart of God? How should we respond to the God who so desires to dwell with His people? It is appropriate that we are compelled to **"come boldly to the throne of grace" (see Hebrews 4:16)** and to **"draw near with a true heart in full assurance of faith" (see Hebrews 10:22).** God's goal in creation is that we would dwell with Him in intimate fellowship. One day we will live with Him in New Jerusalem, the capital city of the universe. May we live in His presence every day until then.

SECTION II:

INTERPRETIVE QUESTIONS, ESCHATOLOGICAL OPINIONS

CHAPTER 9

UNDERSTANDING ESCHATOLOGY

J esus stressed the importance of understanding end-time prophecy. He repeatedly warned us that we must watch for its fulfillment and be ready to respond (see Matthew 24:42-44; 25:13; Mark 13:22-24, 32-37; Luke 21:29-36). With such a clear exhortation from the Lord, we must wholeheartedly pursue understanding of eschatology.

For the past two hundred years, the church has pursued such understanding more than ever. Thousands of books and Bible courses have been devoted to the study of end times. This is an appropriate response to Jesus' exhortations; however, it has led to many varied and conflicting interpretations. Endless opinions have been expressed and countless questions have been raised. How are we to know whose interpretation of end-time Scripture is correct? Is it possible to be confident that we really understand these passages?

There are at least two things we can be confident of. First, we can be confident that every believer can understand the Bible. Wayne Grudem extolls the "clarity of Scripture" in His *Systematic Theology*:

*All the people of Israel were expected to be able to un-
derstand the words of Scripture well enough to be to "teach
them diligently" to their children [see Deuteronomy 6:6-
7]. God expected that all of His people would know and
be able to talk about His Word, with proper application to
ordinary situations in life . . . The character of Scripture
is said to be such that even the "simple" can understand
it rightly and be made wise by it.* **"The testimony of
the Lord is sure, making wise the simple" (Psalm
16:9).** (p. 106)

Further, Paul teaches that the Holy Spirit enables us to, **"know
the things that have been freely given to us by God" (see I
Corinthians 2:6-16).** He encourages Timothy in his pursuit of
understanding God's Word: **"The Holy Scriptures . . . are able
to make you wise for salvation through faith which is in
Christ Jesus. All Scripture is given by inspiration of God,
and is profitable for doctrine, for reproof, for correction,
for instruction in righteousness" (see II Timothy 3:15-16).**
God has given us a Bible that we can understand, with His help.

Second, we can be confident that God will give grace to
the end-time church to understand eschatology. After receiv-
ing his eschatological revelations, Daniel is first told to **"shut
up the words, and seal the book until the time of the
end . . . these words are concealed and sealed up <u>until</u> the
end time"(see Daniel 12:4-10).** The implication is clear: the
understanding of end-time prophecy was sealed and concealed
from generations in the past, but they are being unsealed and
revealed to those living in the end times.

The proceeding chapters will examine the most critical eschatological themes and their various interpretations. We will
attempt to discover a cursory, perhaps even shallow, overview
of each of the major schools of eschatological interpretation

and each major end-time theme. To address them thoroughly would require a much larger volume. In some cases, it will be evident which position the current author holds. In such cases, the goal has been to provide convincing biblical support for these positions.

Schools of Interpretation

Before beginning our examination of the main themes in eschatology, we will survey the various "schools of interpretation" that have shaped the church's understanding of prophetic Scripture. There are several, very different, interpretive models that are applied to "eschatological passages" such as the "Olivet Discourse" (see Matthew 24-25; Luke 21; Mark13), the Book of Daniel, and the Revelation of Jesus Christ. These radically different approaches to the Bible have led to profoundly different interpretations.

Below are the four main schools of interpretation as well as potential strengths and weaknesses of each.

I.   Preterist Interpretation

"Preterist" comes from the Latin *praeter*, which means "past." Preterists believe that the events in so-called pro-phetic passages in the Bible have already happened in the past and are not prophecies of the future. For instance, they approach the Book of Revelation not as a prophecy for the time of the end, but as a message written to the church in John's day. Preterists believe that the destruction of Jerusalem in A.D. 70 fulfilled "day of the Lord" or "last days" passages in prophetic Scripture.

Strengths: There is no doubt that every book of the Bible was, in part, written for the author's contemporary audience. There is truth to be found in studying history to discover what application these books would have had to the original hearers. If we understand the historical context and what the author intended to say to his contemporaries, we make progress in understanding what a text intends to say to our own generation. The "partial preterist" approach is helpful in understanding these things.

Weaknesses: Preterists discount the prophetic (foretelling) nature of Scripture, thus missing any future fulfillment of predictive portions of Scripture. Full preterists believe that even the prophecies of the second coming of Christ and the resurrection of the dead were fulfilled in the past. Thus they believe He has already returned "in His people" and will not return bodily. They believe resurrection passages speak only of spiritual resurrection in the new birth, and that there will be no physical resurrection. These are grave errors that dismiss large portions of Scripture. For this reason, full preterist interpretation of Scripture should be rejected as unbiblical and unorthodox.

II. Historicist Interpretation

Historicists see an "unfolding" of history prophesied in the pages of Scripture. In other words, the Books of Revelation and Daniel were written to prophesy thousands of years of history before it happened. According to this school of interpretation, you can see a timeline of church history. For instance, in the Book of Revelation as a whole you can see the "seven ages of church history" in the seven epistles of Jesus in the beginning of the book.

Strengths: The historicist perspective provides a remarkable way to read prophetic Scripture. It strengthens our faith when we see things accurately prophesied in the Bible. The rise of Catholicism, the Reformation, the birth of America, the conquest of Napoleon, World War II, television, helicopters and planes, and much more have been prophesied in the Bible, according to historicists. The parallels between what is written symbolically in Scripture and historical events that seem to fulfill them are stunning.

Weaknesses: Much of what the Books of Daniel and Revelation prophesy have been fulfilled "in measure" in history, but not in fullness. For instance, the antichrist world ruler who has been prophesied will have a global government, religion, and currency. There have been historic antichrist rulers who have accomplished multinational governmental, religious, and economic leadership, but none have succeeded in true global dominance. There is a danger in historicist interpretation that does not make room for future, total, and literal fulfillments of biblical prophecies. In the next chapter, we will examine how many biblical prophecies have been fulfilled in measure in history but will be ultimately fulfilled in the generation of the Lord's coming.

III. Futurist Interpretation

Futurists consider that many of the prophetic passages in the Gospels, the prophets, and Revelation will have an end-time fulfillment. There are several distinct varieties of futurists, including some who believe in a post-tribulation rapture and others who believe in a pre-tribulation rapture. This means two different futurist scholars could come to very different conclusions.

Strengths: Futurists place great emphasis on the coming of the Lord and the establishment of His kingdom. This is healthy, considering the second coming is one of the most prevalent themes in the entire New Testament. Some futurists believe that many prophecies have had a partial fulfillment in history, but that the ultimate fulfillment of many eschatological passages will happen at the end of the age. This makes room for some synchronization with historicists and even some preterist views.

Weaknesses: As Rick Joyner has said, "You would have to be almost completely ignorant of history to deny that many things in the Book of Revelation have been fulfilled in history." There are futurists who dogmatically assert that historicists and preterists are simply "wrong" in their interpretations, rather than acknowledging the legitimacy of some of their perspectives. If we cannot recognize how prophetic Scripture has been fulfilled in history, we will not be equipped to understand future fulfillments either. Dogmatism about the non-essentials of the faith stunts our spiritual growth and constrains us to a myopic view of Scripture.

IV. Idealist Interpretation

Idealists read so-called prophetic Scripture not as a prophecy of the future or eschatological events. Instead, they read it to discover "timeless truths" or "ideals" that apply to every generation in every situation. In other words, the Book of Revelation was not about Rome and the first-century church, nor is about the end-time antichrist and the victorious end-time church—it's about the timeless struggle between good and evil, or between God and the devil.

Strengths: It is true that every book of the Bible is written for all people, times, and situations. Idealists may catch overarching themes in prophetic Scripture that are missed by others who are too focused on minute details. If we are too consumed with finding the identity of the woman in Revelation 12 for example, we may miss the point: The dragon's fierce attack fails and God supernaturally protects.

Idealists catch these pertinent messages in eschatological texts.

Weaknesses: Idealists miss some of the most important characteristics of Scripture. The Book of Revelation, for instance, is called **"the words of this prophecy" (see Revelation 1:3; 22:7-19)**, meaning that the book is prophetic and concerned with the future. Revelation 1:19 says the book concerns **"what is now"** as well as what **"will take place after this"**—a biblical idiom referring to the end-times. As we saw previously, Daniel 12:4 and 12:9 explicitly reveal that the book is for "the time of the end." If we do not allow eschatological books like Revelation, Daniel, and Zechariah to prophesy of the future, we miss their primary purpose.

Conclusion

Most teachers of eschatology hold firmly to one of these four schools of interpretation, while thoroughly rejecting the others. The problem with such a rigid posture is that in some cases, convincing interpretations can be provided from the opposing schools. Is it possible that each of these schools could be accurately seeing something about prophetic Scripture? Or, is it best to adopt one of the above positions, wholesale? I believe the answers to these questions are found in an examination of the supernatural nature of Scripture, which we will undertake in the next chapter.

CHAPTER 10
SUPERNATURAL SCRIPTURE

The Word of God is living and active; it is supernatural. In the natural order, words can only affect the physical world when accompanied by action. When God speaks, however, His spoken Word releases the power to accomplish His intention. Isaiah 55:10-11 tells us, **"As the rain comes down, and the snow from heaven, and do not return there, but water the earth, and make it bring forth and bud . . . So shall My word be that goes forth from My mouth; it shall not return to Me void, but it shall accomplish what I please, and it shall prosper in the thing for which I sent it."** In other words, just like rain and snow water the earth and cause it to produce fruit, God's Word impacts creation and produces the very thing that He spoke. His Word has creative power to bring forth His will.

Let's consider prophetic Scripture in light of this principle. God has declared His intention for the future through His spoken and written Word. His intention will surely come to pass because His Word has creative power. However, there are some things He spoke thousands of years ago that will not be fully realized until the second coming of Christ (or even beyond). Does that mean these Words of God will remain "inactive" until their time of ultimate fulfillment? Or did some of these

Divine dictates begin to impact history immediately after He spoke them to the prophets?

Searching for *Sensus Plenoire*

It seems that some biblical prophecies were fulfilled "in measure" soon after they were spoken, yet a future eschatological fulfillment remains. There are even some instances in Scripture and history where a prophecy was fulfilled "in measure" over and over again. The future, ultimate fulfillment or *sensus plenoire* (Latin for "fullest sense") of such prophecies will likely come forth in the generation of the Lord's coming. Consider such biblical predictions as the coming of antichrist or the coming of Elijah before the day of the Lord (see Daniel 7-12; II Thessalonians 2:3; I John 2:18; Malachi 4:5).

In the case of the antichrist, contemporaries would have assumed Alexander the Great was the beast-man Daniel spoke of as he conquered the civilized world. Two hundred years later, Antiochus Epiphanies appeared to be the antichrist performing the abomination of desolation as he ransacked Jerusalem and sacrificed a pig on the altar in of the temple. However, Jesus made it clear nearly two hundred years afterwards that the abomination of desolation was still future (see Matthew 24:15). Many in history such as Nero, Napoleon, and Adolf Hitler partially fulfilled antichrist prophecies as well. Nevertheless, no single person has yet fulfilled *all* that is written of the "man of sin." John explains, ***"The Antichrist is coming, even now many antichrists have come"*** *(see I John 2:18)*. In other words, many have walked in the **"spirit of the Antichrist" (see I John 4:3)** and partially fulfilled the prophecies, yet one will come in the future who will fulfill them all.

As for the coming of Elijah, Jesus told us that John the Baptist at least partially fulfilled Malachi 4:5 as he prepared the way for the Lord. However, many believe that God is releasing the "spirit of Elijah" upon the end-time church to prepare the way for the second coming of Jesus—walking in Elijah-like signs and wonders and turning **"the hearts of the fathers to the children, and the hearts of the children to their fathers"(see Malachi 4:6).** Still others believe Elijah will return bodily as one of the two witnesses.

It seems that the above are examples of a single prophecy having multiple "partial fulfillments" prior to the *sensus plenoire*. It could also be said that these various historic events "foreshadow" the prophecies without conclusively fulfilling them. Let's further examine this phenomenon of prophetic Scripture having layers of interpretation and fulfillment.

Layers of Fulfillment

Have you ever been perplexed by the sweeping scope of prophetic Scripture? Have you noticed how a prophet can speak of two events in the same breath that will actually take place hundreds or thousands of years apart from one another? In such instances, the prophet usually gives no indication that his prophecy encompasses alternating epochs of time. Consider Zechariah 9:9-10:

> **"Rejoice greatly, O daughter of Zion! Shout, O daughter of Jerusalem! Behold, your King is coming to you; He is just and having salvation, lowly and riding on a donkey, a colt, the foal of a donkey.**
> **"I will cut off the chariot from Ephraim and the horse from Jerusalem; the battle bow shall be cut off. He shall speak peace to the nations; His**

dominion shall be 'from sea to sea, and from the River to the ends of the earth.'"

Verse 9 of this Messianic prophecy certainly speaks of the first coming of Jesus; He was celebrated as King when He rode into Jerusalem on the colt of a donkey (see Luke 19:35-38). However, the very next verse is obviously speaking of the second coming of Jesus, when He will put an end to war and establish His dominion from sea to sea. Apparently, Zechariah saw these two events that span thousands of years overlapping one another in a single vision. This vision has more than one layer of fulfillment.

Consider also Isaiah 7:14, a verse that has provoked some controversy through the years:

Therefore the Lord Himself will give you a sign: Behold, the virgin shall conceive and bear a Son, and shall call His name Immanuel.

Most Bible versions translate the Hebrew word *almah* in Isaiah 7:14 as "virgin" while others translate it as "young woman." This is because the word has a wide semantic range and can speak of either a virgin or a young woman. When Isaiah initially gave this prophecy, he was speaking to King Ahaz of a sign God would give to him. He was most likely speaking of his own wife in the immediate context, a young woman who would soon have a child—whose name would be a prophecy to King Ahaz and Israel (see Isaiah 8:3-4). However, more than seven hundred years later, Matthew picked up this prophecy and applied it to Mary, the mother of Jesus (see Matthew 1:23). Matthew interprets *almah* in Isaiah 7:14 as "virgin" and he understands the verse as a prophecy of the immaculate conception.

Could it be that Isaiah's prophecy was a *kairos* word for King Ahaz, yet it was also a prediction of the virgin birth hundreds of years in the future? Evidently this prophecy had more than one layer of fulfillment, and so do many other biblical prophecies.

A Key to Unlock Prophetic Scripture

The above concept can serve as a revolutionary paradigm for interpreting prophetic Scripture. God's power is at work to fulfill everything He has spoken. Therefore, we often see prophecy fulfilled in-measure in successive generations. This concept is a key to unlocking prophetic Scripture. It is also a key to understanding the different and often convincing approaches to eschatology.

In *Of Angels, Beasts, and Plagues*, Kenneth Maahs wrestles with the relevance of two seemingly antithetical schools of biblical interpretation: the partial preterist view, which is concerned with first-century fulfillments of prophecy, and the futurist view, which is concerned with end-time fulfillment of prophecy. He writes, "Both are consistent interpretations, and each yields a powerful message for the church of any era. But how can both be possible? Can a book of the Bible mean two different things at the same time?" Ultimately, a book of the Bible cannot mean two different things at the same time, as that would violate the logical principle of non-contradiction. A book can, however, have two layers of interpretation.

Below is a modified version of a diagram from *How to Read the Bible for All It's Worth*, by Gordon Fee and Doug Stuart:

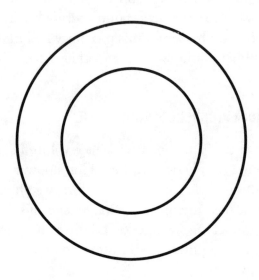

INITIAL PERSPECTIVE OF A PROPHECY

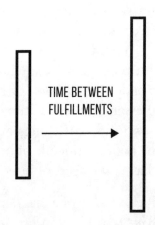

TIME BETWEEN
FULFILLMENTS

**SAME PROPHECY VIEWED WITH THE
PERSPECTIVE OF HISTORY**

Biblical prophetic literature is like these discs. At first glance, some passages appear to be speaking of a single future event (like when viewing these discs from the front, they appear as one object). However, with the perspective of history and sound hermeneutics, we see that such prophecies are speaking of more than a single event (like when viewing these discs from the side, you can see they are separate objects with distance between them). This is the case with Zechariah 9:9-10, Isaiah 7:14, and the prophecies of the antichrist. These and many other passages will have more than one fulfillment, often with a significant span of time in-between.

Consider the diagram above in light of Isaiah 55:10-11. God's Word is sent from heaven like raindrops into the waters of history, causing concentric ripples throughout all of time. Just as ripples in a body of water multiply until they reach the shore, God's prophetic utterance initiates more than one fulfillment (in some cases), and then culminates in the *sensus plenior*.

This principle explains how each of the diverse schools of interpretation discussed in chapter 9 can sometimes set forth profound revelation of Scripture. God's Word is supernatural and it is possible for a single Bible prophecy to: have an application for the prophet's own generation and ripple through time, influencing history, *and* culminate in an end-time fulfillment.

Perhaps, the fullest understanding of eschatology is to observe the Word of the Lord moving in power through many generations toward its ultimate last-day fruition.

Already And Not Yet

The annals of eschatology preserve a potent trope, "already, and not yet." This phrase elucidates many paradoxes in the Word of God. We are "already" saved when we are born again, but we are "not yet" fully saved (from all the influence of the world, the flesh, and the devil) until the kingdom of God comes. Satan has "already" been defeated at the resurrection of Christ, but he has "not yet" been fully annihilated, as he will be in the lake of fire (see Revelation 20:10). We have "already" been healed by the finished work of the cross, but we have "not yet" experienced the fullness of our glorified bodies. We live in an interesting epoch—an "age between the ages." Jesus has already come, but the fullness of His dominion will not be seen until His second advent.

This "already, not yet" way of looking at prophetic Scripture is sometimes called "inaugurated eschatology." This paradigm says that the kingdom of God was inaugurated at the time of the outpouring of the Holy Spirit at Pentecost. Thus, we can begin to experience Christ's victory, power, and glory now, in measure. The fullness is still to come, yet everything prophesied in Scripture of the coming kingdom can manifest in our present age—in measure.

When the Lord establishes His throne, there will be no more war, no more sin, no more sickness, no more devil. Therefore, everywhere we manifest the kingdom there will be peace, righteousness, healing, and dominion over the enemy—in increasing measure, as we approach the end of the age. As Derek Prince states in *Shaping History Through Fasting and Prayer,* "the supernatural gifts of the Holy Spirit . . . are to be more and more manifested the nearer we come to the end of the age." We can "already" see the kingdom coming, though it has "not yet" filled the earth.

God's powerful Word has given us faith and access to many of these "already" kingdom-realities. The "not yet" aspects of the kingdom will surely come because His Word "will accomplish that which He sent it forth to do" (see Isaiah 55:10-11)!

Perhaps the most effective way to interpret prophetic Scripture is to consider it as "living and active" (see Hebrews 4:12) and multifaceted in application. The Word of the Lord is supernatural—powerful enough to shape and determine history ahead of time.

CHAPTER 11

GREAT ESCHATOLOGICAL THEMES PART I

Hunger and Humility

There are endless theories concerning the sequence and specifics of end-time events. Talk of the last days may bring to mind cluttered charts and timelines. We may have heard dogmatic delineations of the various schools of interpretation—each claiming that theirs is the historic doctrine, the one taught by the early church fathers. Truth be told, you can find nearly any theory written somewhere in the first several hundred years of church history.

Considering all of the above, humility is paramount in our approach to eschatology. There are certain end-time themes that are clearly expounded in Scripture. There are others, however, that are ethereal and nuanced. Let us determine not to be dogmatic in our approach to these, but to advance with open minds and hungry hearts.

Understanding Eschatology

Jesus expects us to understand the signs of the times (see Matthew 16:4) and to be ready for His coming (see Luke 12:40). This is why we take the study of eschatology seriously. There is great reward for such study: obtaining **"the revelation of Jesus Christ" (see Revelation 1:1).** Above all else, we want to know Him and His glorious plan for **"the restoration of all things" (see Acts 3:21).** This and the following chapter will explore several of the main features of that glorious plan and the various ways they have been interpreted.

These chapters will only be able to cover a brief overview of these central eschatological themes. The main interpretive positions on these themes will be examined, with the goal of providing a succinct but accurate summary of each. The position held by the author will be evident, however, and previous chapters will often be referenced to clarify these positions.

The Timing of the Second Coming of Jesus and the Rapture

The New Testament clearly teaches a physical, bodily return of Jesus to earth (see Acts 1:11; I Thessalonians 4:16; Matthew 24:30-31). Further, although the word "rapture" is not in the Bible, the New Testament does speak of believers being "caught up" in the air to meet Jesus when He returns (see Matthew 24:30-31; I Thessalonians 4:17). It is at the time of the return of Christ and "rapture" of the church that believers receive their glorified bodies (see I Corinthians 15:51-52; I John 3:2). There are three main views concerning the timing of these events. They are the pre-tribulation, mid-tribulation, and post-tribulation views. There are nuances within each of these views that may vary from teacher to teacher, but we will attempt to examine the core teaching of each view.

Many teachers of eschatology speak of a seven year period preceding the second coming of the Lord. This is often referred to as the great tribulation. Some teach that the first three and a half of the seven years are called the tribulation and the last three and a half years are called the great tribulation. The seven year period of time is taken from Daniel's prophecy of a seven year covenant made between the antichrist and many nations (see Daniel 9:27). The seven year period is divided into two three and a half year halves because Daniel (and Jesus) speak of a significant shift in the middle of the seven year period brought about by the **"abomination of desolation" (see Daniel 9:27, 12:11; Matthew 24:15)**, and because many end-time passages speak of the final forty-two months, or one thousand two hundred and sixty days, of history as a distinct block of time (see Revelation 11:2-3, 12:6, 13:5; Daniel 7:25, 12:7, 12:11).

We will now examine the three main views of the timing of the return of Christ and rapture of the church. What follows is:

1. A brief summary of each view
2. An exploration of some of the proof texts for each view
3. A possible refutation of each view

I. Pre-tribulation Rapture

Proponents of this view teach that Jesus will rapture the church secretly "like a thief in the night" *before* (or pre-) the great tribulation. Jesus will take the church back to heaven in their newly received glorified bodies for seven years. During these seven years on earth, the antichrist will reign and will persecute all who do not yield to his authority *and* God will release the judgments of the Book of Revelation. As a result of this persecution and judgment, many Jews and Gentiles will be born again as they turn to Jesus for salvation. Jesus will return again to the earth (visibly this time) at the end of seven years with an army of saints to fight the last battle of Revelation 19 and to establish His kingdom.

The doctrine of a pre-tribulation or "pre-trib" rapture is a relatively new teaching. The first clear articulation of this teaching came from John Nelson Darby, who is considered the father of dispensationalism, in the 1830s. Some of Darby's contemporaries suggested his teaching on the rapture was influenced by Margaret MacDonald's 1830 vision of the end-times. Modern proponents of pre-tribulationism refute this, however. The pre-tribulation rapture was widely popularized by the 1909 *C.I. Scofield Reference Bible*. This was the principal study Bible of the early 20th century and it incorporated Darby's doctrine in the study notes.

Pre-tribulation Rapture "Proof Texts" and Refutations:

#1: I Thessalonians 5:2: "the day of the Lord so comes as a thief in the night."

This verse is used to emphasize the "secret coming" of the Lord to rapture the church, prior to His coming with the army of saints seven years later.

Refutation: In context, this passage is a warning to those who are in darkness; it is not a description of the rapture. Paul writes to Thessalonian believers, **"But you, brethren, are not in darkness, so that this Day should overtake you as a thief"** (verse 4). In other words, for believers, His coming will not be like a thief in the night.

The **"thief in the night"** terminology does not speak of a secret coming, but a violent robbery. Those who are not ready for the coming of the Lord will suffer great loss. In speaking of the "day of the Lord," Paul is using the Old

Testament language for the great conflict that takes place on earth when Jesus returns to overthrow evil by His wrath.

#2: I Thessalonians 5:9: "God did not appoint us to wrath, but to obtain salvation."

This verse is interpreted as, "God has not appointed us (believers) to wrath, and therefore we will not be on earth during the great tribulation."

Refutation: In I Thessalonians 5, Paul is making a distinction between believers who are appointed to salvation and unbelievers who are appointed to wrath—if they do not repent. Believers who are on the earth during the tribulation will not be under (or appointed to) God's wrath. They will be instruments of God's grace and mercy, bright lights in the darkest darkness, calling men and women to repent and receive salvation. It will be the greatest hour for the church.

Further, the use of this verse to support a pre-tribulation rapture assumes that God's sole purpose in the tribulation is to express His wrath, however it is not. God also purposes to bring repentance and thus salvation to as many people as possible during the tribulation (see "Christ's Messianic Resolution" in chapter 4).

#3: Luke 17:34-36: "I tell you, in that night there will be two men in one bed: the one will be taken and the other will be left. Two women will be grinding together: the one will be taken and the other left. Two men will be in the field: the one will be taken and the other left."

Pre-tribulationists reference this passage to illustrate the "secret rapture" of the church. This imagery was vividly portrayed in the *Left Behind* series. Jesus catches the church away and millions of people disappear with no explanation. Unbelievers who are left on earth do not see the coming of Jesus and thus are completely confused as to where the missing individuals have gone.

Refutation: This passage does speak of the rapture of the church, but it does not comment as to when the rapture happens. If Jesus returns at the end of the tribulation, the verse still makes logical sense. There will still be one person taken from a bed or a field and another left behind—after the tribulation.

Further, several passages are clear that when Jesus comes again **"every eye will see Him" (see Revelation 1:7).** Matthew 24:30-31 explicitly tells us that all nations will see Him as He gathers His elect (Christians) to meet Him in the sky.

II. Mid-Tribulation Rapture

The mid-tribulation doctrine of the rapture is certainly the minority view. Proponents of this view divide the final seven years into two halves: the tribulation, which consists of the wrath of Satan and the persecution of the church, and the great tribulation, which consists of the wrath of God and judgment of evil. This position teaches that Jesus visibly appears in the sky and raptures the church at the three and a half year mark. He then takes the church in their newly glorified bodies to heaven for the remaining three and a half years. During this three and a half years on earth, the greatest tribulation occurs and the wrath of God is poured out. At the end of the final three and a half years, Jesus returns to earth with an army of glorified saints to fight the battle of Revelation 19, and establish His kingdom on earth.

There are variations of this view, including the "pre-wrath" rapture position, which is somewhat of a synthesis of the mid-tribulation and post-tribulation rapture positions. This position, which appeared at the end of the 20th century, does not propose that the rapture necessarily happens at the three and a half year mark. They propose that the church goes through at least three and a half of the seven years and that *whatever* subsequent time the rapture occurs, it marks the beginning of "the day of the Lord" or the "wrath of God." "Pre-wrath" proponents do not purport to know the precise timing of the rapture—only that it is during the second half of the seven years, directly before God pours out the fullness of His wrath.

Mid-tribulation Rapture "Proof Texts" and Refutations:

#1: Revelation 12:12: "Therefore rejoice, O heavens, and you who dwell in them! Woe to the inhabitants of the earth and the sea! For the devil has come down to you, having great wrath, because he knows that he has a short time."

This verse is understood to delineate the wrath of Satan as the first three and a half years of tribulation. The idiom **"a short time"** is understood as an indirect reference to the phrase **"time and times, and half a time"** from Daniel 7:25, that indicates three and a half years. This is emphasized because the final three and a half years is understood to be reserved for the wrath of God. The argument is made that the rapture must take place when the years of the devil's "great wrath" is complete and before the three and a half years of God's wrath begins, since **"God did not appoint** [believers] **to wrath"** (see I Thessalonians 5:9).

Refutation: As stated above, if Christians are still on earth during the final three and a half years of the great tribulation, they still will not be appointed to wrath. If God is pouring out His wrath on the antichrist's empire, anointed believers will be the mouthpiece of God calling all who remain to repentance and salvation (see "A People of Power Like the World Has Never Seen" in chapter 3 for more on this). Further, God's wrath is poured out during the *final* judgment series in the Book of Revelation, the seven bowls of wrath. This seems to occur near the close of the seven years, rather than at the halfway point. The bowls of wrath are poured out after the seven seal judgments (see Revelation 6, 8:1-6) and after the seven trumpet judgments (see Revelation 8:7-13, 9, 11:15-19). For a discussion of possible timespans of the judgment events in the Book of Revelation, see chapter 5, "The Battle for the Kingdom."

#2: Revelation 6:12-7:14: "I looked when He opened the sixth seal, and behold, there was a great earthquake; and the sun became black as sackcloth of hair, and the moon became like blood. And the stars of heaven fell to the earth, as a fig tree drops its late figs when it is shaken by a mighty wind . . . After these things I looked, and behold, a great multitude which no one could number, of all nations, tribes, peoples, and tongues, standing before the throne and before the Lamb, clothed with white robes . . . "Who are these arrayed in white robes, and where did they come from?" And I said to him, "Sir, you know." So he said to me, "These are the ones who come out of the great tribulation, and washed their robes and made them white in the blood of the Lamb."

This passage is considered by mid-tribulationists to show that the rapture of the church takes place directly before the final three and a half years begins. The first three verses (6:12-14) are distinctly parallel to Matthew 24:29, a passage that clearly describes the rapture:

"The sun will be darkened, and the moon will not give its light; the stars will fall from heaven, and the powers of the heavens will be shaken."

These three verses also parallel Isaiah 13:9-10, which describes the day of the Lord, or the day of His **"wrath and fierce anger:"**

"Behold, the day of the LORD comes, cruel, with both wrath and fierce anger, to lay the land desolate . . . "For the stars of heaven and their constellations will not give their light; the sun will be darkened in its going forth, and the moon will not cause its light to shine."

Further, according to this interpretation, Revelation 7:9-14 describes a great multitude who have just been raptured. They are standing before the throne in white robes from all over the earth and they have just **"come out of the great tribulation" (see Revelation 7:14).**

In summary, mid-tribulationists consider that Revelation 6:12-7:14 shows that the rapture coincides with the beginning of the day of the Lord—which they understand to be the final three and a half years of history before the Christ's return.

Refutation: Many interpreters consider that the Book of Revelation is not entirely chronological. It contains chronological sections, which are identified by the chronological sequences of the seven seals, seven trumpets, and seven bowls of wrath. It also contains obvious parenthetical sections, which give explanation to the chronological sections.

In the above passage, Revelation 6:12-17 concludes the chronological narrative of the "seven seals." However, chapter 7 is a parenthesis that is meant to answer the question asked at the end of chapter 6, **"For the great day of His wrath has come and who is able to stand?"** Chapter 7 answers the question by describing 144,000 children of Israel marked by God (see 7:4-9), and a countless number of Gentiles who have washed their garments white in the blood of the Lamb (see 7:9-17). These will "stand" throughout the prophesied Day of Judgment. Therefore, the **"great multitude that no one can number"** is not a picture of the rapture necessarily; it is a picture of the great harvest of souls who will accept Christ and receive eternal life during the great tribulation.

There are many diverse approaches to mid-tribulation teaching and the above is an attempt to highlight a few main arguments. However, it is difficult to pinpoint a unifying and comprehensive account of this doctrine.

III. Post-Tribulation Rapture

The post-tribulation rapture doctrine teaches that the church will be on the earth during the great tribulation. This time of tribulation will not be a time of destruction for believers, but it will be our greatest hour. During the great tribulation, God will release judgments on the earth in order to bring mankind to repentance (see Revelation 9:20-21, 16:9-11) so that He can save them. The church will walk in great power during this time, displaying the power of the coming kingdom of God with miracles, signs, and wonders. This power will enable them to partner with Jesus to bring in the end-time harvest of souls

Great Eschatological Themes Part I

(see Matthew 13:39; Revelation 14:14-16). At the end of the great tribulation, Jesus will return from heaven riding on the clouds to rapture the church and confront the antichrist and his armies.

Post-tribulation Rapture "Proof Texts" and Refutations:

#1: Matthew 24:21-31: "For then there will be <u>great tribulation</u>, such as has not been since the beginning of the world until this time, no, nor ever shall be.

And unless those days were shortened, no flesh would be saved; but for the elect's sake those days will be shortened . . . <u>Immediately after the tribulation of those days</u> the sun will be darkened, and the moon will not give its light; the stars will fall from heaven, and the powers of the heavens will be shaken. Then the sign of the Son of Man will appear in heaven, and then all the tribes of the earth will mourn, and they will see the Son of Man coming on the clouds of heaven with power and great glory. And He will send His angels with a great sound of a trumpet, and they will gather together His elect from the four winds, from one end of heaven to the other."

This passage is from "The Olivet Discourse," Jesus' most comprehensive treatise on the **"the sign of [His] coming, and of the end of the age" (see 24:3).** Verse 21 is where we get the phrase "the great tribulation." Jesus describes this period of tribulation, which precedes His coming, and then He plainly states that **"immediately after the tribulation of those days"** the Son of Man will appear in heaven and the whole earth will see Him coming on the clouds with power and great glory. At the same time the angels will gather the saints from the four winds to meet Him in the sky (see 24:29-31). This passage is a definite statement of the timing of the second coming of Jesus and the rapture the church. It takes place *after* the great tribulation.

Refutation: Pre-tribulationists disagree that this is a picture of the rapture and the second coming. They would suggest that it is only a picture of the second coming, since they believe the rapture will be a "secret coming" and that He will not be seen by "all the tribes of the earth." Therefore, they say the second coming is after the great tribulation, but the rapture is not. The problem with their interpretation, however, is that Matthew 24:31 speaks of the trumpet. The trumpet is explicitly linked to the rapture of the church in I Corinthians 15:51-52 and several other passages (see below).

#2: I Corinthians 15:51-52: "Behold, I tell you a mystery: We shall not all sleep, but we shall all be changed—in a moment, in the twinkling of an eye, at <u>the last trumpet</u>. For the trumpet will sound, and the dead will be raised incorruptible, and we shall be changed." (See also: Revelation 11:15-19; Matthew 24:31; I Thessalonians 4:16.)

Post-tribulationists identify the "trumpet motif" in second coming passages as an indicator of the timing of the rapture and second coming. I Corinthians 15:51 teaches that the rapture takes place at the sound of the last trumpet. The idea of a "secret rapture" is rejected, in consideration of passages like Matthew 24:30, **"then all the tribes of the earth will mourn, and they will see the Son of Man coming on the clouds of heaven with power and great glory,"** and Revelation 1:7, **"Behold, He is coming with clouds, and every eye will see Him."** Everyone will see Jesus when He returns. There are not two future comings of the Lord—one for the rapture and one for the second coming—they are one event. Matthew 24:29-31 is clear: Jesus' coming on the clouds, appearance to the whole earth, and gathering of the church to meet Him in the air all occur simultaneously. The second coming of Jesus and the rapture both take place at the sound of the last trumpet.

The "last trumpet" found in the Bible is in Revelation 11:15-19, the seventh trumpet. (For the vivid second coming imagery of the trumpet motif, see "The Trumpet and the Coming of the King" in chapter 4). At this point in Revelation, six of the seven trumpet judgments have already been released. Only the seven bowl judgments remain, and unlike many of the seal and trumpet judgments, these can be accomplished in a succinct period of time. This places the last trumpet and corresponding second coming and rapture shortly before the battle of Armageddon and at the end of the great tribulation. For a detailed discussion of the timing of these events, see chapter 5 "The Battle for the Kingdom."

Refutation: As with proof text #1, since pre-tribulationists teach two future comings of the Lord (the rapture and His bodily return), they interpret I Corinthians 15:51-52 as describing the rapture and not the second coming. They would, therefore, not see the "last trumpet" as an indicating a post-tribulational rapture. Nevertheless, there appears to be no adequate refutation for the implications of the consolidated "trumpet" references in second coming passages.

Conclusion

The topic of the timing of the rapture and second coming of the Lord has been a point of contention for many years, but things are changing. More and more people are embracing the doctrine of the victorious end-time church, who will be present on earth during the great end-time tribulation. According to Acts 14:22, **"through many tribulations we enter the kingdom of God,"** and it appears that the whole church and the earth enter into the great kingdom age through the great tribulation.

Regardless of someone's position on this doctrine, it is evident from Jesus' teaching that the time before His coming will be an unprecedented time of trial and shaking. He describes many difficult things that come upon the earth during the "the beginning of sorrows" (or "beginning of birth pangs"). Regardless of one's position on the rapture, we can all be absolutely certain the church will go through these events. It is for this reason we are told to "watch" and "be on alert" (see Matthew 24:42, 25:13; Mark 13:34-37; Luke 21:36) so that we will be prepared for His coming.

We must take these New Testament exhortations seriously:

But the end of all things is at hand; therefore be serious and watchful in your prayers (I Peter 4:7).

Watch, stand fast in the faith, be brave, be strong (I Corinthians 16:13).

Therefore let us not sleep, as others do, but let us watch and be sober (I Thessalonians 5:6).

CHAPTER 12
GREAT ESCHATOLOGICAL THEMES PART II

Let's continue our study of great eschatological themes by considering two more important topics: the antichrist and the millennial reign of Jesus. As stated in the previous chapter, below is only a cursory discussion of these vast topics.

Who or What is the Antichrist?

Is the antichrist a person or an evil world system?

There are three main views of who or what the antichrist is. These views vary widely, and they have a weighty impact on how we understand eschatological Scripture. Below is an examination of the three main views:

#1: The antichrist is not a person, but an evil world system. According to this view, the word "antichrist" signifies an increasingly anti-Christ and anti-Christian world system in which we live. Passages that speak of the "antichrist" (see I John 2:18), "beast" (see Revelation 13:14), **"man of lawlessness" (see II Thessalonians 2:3)**, or "horn" (see Daniel 7:21) are understood to efer to evil in general or to some specific historical context. Those who hold this view are not expecting a future

evil world ruler to arise and establish a global government, economy, military, and religion.

The problem with this view is that the antichrist is spoken of as an individual in many places. He is referred to as the ***man* of lawlessness" (see II Thessalonians 2:3)**, he is called a contemptible person (see Daniel 11:21), he blasphemes (see Revelation 13:5-6), he speaks (see Daniel 7:25), and he does many other "personal" things. John tells us there is a "spirit of antichrist" which is behind many evil world systems (see I John 4:3, 2:18), but there is also a single "antichrist" (see I John 2:18) who will come at the time of the end.

The anti-Christ is the antithesis to Christ. Christ is a real person. He will be King of the nations, will be worshipped by all, will sit on His throne in Jerusalem—and Satan has planned for the antichrist to do each of these things as well. He will even scam the world with what appears to be this false Christ's death and subsequent resurrection (see Revelation 13:3). It is after his resurrection that the world begins to marvel and to worship him (see Revelation 13:4). Sounds familiar, right? The evidence seems to weigh heavily in favor of the antichrist being an actual person just as Christ is an actual person.

#2: *The antichrist is the pope, the head of the Catholic church.* This view can be found in history as early as the 10th century, but Martin Luther and other reformers popularized it during the 17th century. There is a striking parallel between some Roman Catholic history and the prophecies of the great harlot Babylon and the antichrist.

For example, in Revelation 17, the harlot is seen as one who sits on many waters, signifying her influence with many nations. The masses drink from her cup and become drunk with the wine of her idolatry (abominations) and martyrdom (the blood of the saints). The Catholic church was responsible for the promulgation of pagan practices within Christendom and for martyring many believers who would not bow their knee to the pope. Further, the harlot is seen riding on the back of the beast (one of the symbolic names for antichrist in Revelation). This would signify the Catholic religion being carried and upheld by the Papal office. ers who would not bow their knee to the pope. Further, the harlot is seen riding on the back of the beast (one of the symbolic names for antichrist in Revelation). This would signify the Catholic religion being carried and upheld by the Papal office.

We are told in II Thessalonians 2:4 that the antichrist **"exalts himself above all that is called God or that is worshiped, so that he sits as God in the temple of God, showing himself that he is God."** Many in church history saw the pope as doing exactly this. His claim to authority on par with Scripture and the anonym of "holy father" have been considered blasphemous. The church is the temple of God and only the Godhead is worthy to be exalted there.

It appears that the pope and the historic Catholic church have sometimes foreshadowed a coming antichrist and great harlot. However, there have also been genuine moves of God in the Catholic church that looked more like heaven on earth than an antichrist empire. There have even been popes that were sincere and godly leaders—much more like Christ than the antichrist. Finally, many "antichrist" prophecies were never fulfilled by the papacy or the Catholic church. For example, no time in Catholic history fulfills Revelation 17:16-17, when the beast and the other kings hate the harlot and violently destroy her.

#3: *The antichrist will be a literal Satan-empowered human being.* As stated above, the passages in Scripture that speak of the antichrist, the man of sin, the little horn, the beast, appear to describe a single individual. We are told that

113

he will lead a global rebellion against Jesus at the culmination of history. If these prophetic passages are taken literally, we can expect this end-time leader to establish a global government (see Daniel 7:23; Revelation 13:7), a global economy (see Revelation 13:16-17), and a global religion (see Revelation 17). His primary goal will be to rule the nations of the earth from Jerusalem and to be worshipped by them. He is the *anti*-Christ, or the antithesis of Christ, and he will seek to usurp the role that Father God has ordained for His Son.

The Millennial Reign of Christ

There are also three main views of the millennial reign of Christ: pre-millennial, post-millennial, and a-millennial. A person's position on this topic has massive implications for their overall understanding of eschatology. It not only impacts what we believe about the millennium, but also what we believe about kingdom of God, the second coming of Christ, and the end times—the years preceding His return. Below are the three main views on this topic. (See chapters 6 and 7 for further discussion on the millennium.)

#1: Pre-millennial: Jesus will return before the millennial kingdom begins. According to this view, **"the kingdoms of this world have become the kingdoms of our Lord and of His Christ" (see Revelation 11:15)** at the second coming of Christ. Jesus will then establish His kingly reign on the earth, alongside many resurrected saints who will be His princes and governors (see Luke 19:17-19; II Timothy 2:12; Revelation 5:10; Revelation 20:4). He will oversee a one thousand year period of restoration, preparing the way for God the Father to come to earth (see Revelation 21:3-7). The premillennial view assumes a literal interpretation of Revelation 19 and 20.

This is the majority view among evangelicals; however, there are several variations of pre-millennialism. For instance, within historic pre-millennialism many teach a victorious end-time church and a post-tribulation return of Christ. On the other hand, dispensational pre-millennialism, a different pre-millennial paradigm, typically assumes a pre-tribulation return of Christ.

#2: Post-millennial: Jesus will return to the earth after the millennial kingdom has been completed. According to this view, the one thousand year period of Revelation 20:2 is a future era (not necessarily a literal thousand years) in which the earth will be mostly Christianized. Christ will reign from heaven through His people first, before returning physically to the earth. The accomplishment of the Great Commission fulfills the prophecies of Satan being bound (see Revelation 20:2) and the saints reigning with Jesus (see Revelation 20:4). Thus, we may already be in some stage of the millennium and things will get better and better on earth, until it is prepared for the second coming of Jesus.

Since post-millennialists believe that the earth will be more and more Christianized until Christ's return, the idea of a future great tribulation is rejected. The post-millennial interpretation of Scripture is preterist by nature; meaning that they consider the so-called "end-time" prophecies of Scripture to have been fulfilled in the past. The destruction of Jerusalem in 70 A.D. fulfilled the prophecies of tribulation by Daniel, Jesus, and John in Revelation.

There are several objections to this view. Chief among them are the numerous passages that speak of a time of trouble preceding the second coming of Christ (see Daniel 7:9-8; Matthew 24; II Thessalonians 2:1-3; Revelation 3-19). The end-time trouble portrayed in these passages seems to contradict the notion that things get better and better preceding the second coming.

#3: A-millennial: there is no future one thousand year reign of Christ. According to this view, the one thousand year period in Revelation 20:2 is figurative language to describe the present church age that began at Pentecost. Jesus is now reigning over the earth from heaven and similar to the post-millennial view, the prophecies of Satan being "bound" and saints "reigning on earth" are fulfilled in the accomplishment of the Great Commission during this age. In contrast to the post-millennial view, a-millennialists are not expecting the whole earth to be Christianized before the second coming.

Biblical objections to this view are evident. At the forefront are many passages of Scripture that seem to be incongruent with both the present church age and the eternal age to come. These include Zechariah 8:22-23 *and* Isaiah 11:6-9, 61:4-9, and 65:20-25. These describe a unique time in history when Jesus will reign over an earth populated by both resurrected saints and people in natural bodies who live for hundreds of years. Babies will be born and people will die—yet Jesus will be on the earth bodily. This unique timeframe is clearly distinct from the present church age.

Further, Satan is certainly not yet bound, **"so that he should deceive the nations no more" (see Revelation 20:3).** The New Testament highlights deception as a hallmark of the last days (see Mark 13:5-6; II Thessalonians 2:3; I John 4:1; Revelation 16:14-15). Only after the return of Christ and His overthrow of evil will Satan's deception be put to an end. If Satan is already bound in this age, then how are we to understand the existence of witchcraft, child abuse, murder, suicide, and a thousand other evils?

Finally, in the present age, the saints are not yet resurrected and reigning with Christ in the way Revelation 20:4-6 describes. Resurrection power is available to us and we "reign with Christ" in a spiritual sense, but Revelation 20:1-4 appears to describe something more.

Conclusion

Innumerable volumes of theology have been written to wrestle over these and other important end-time themes. The Bible's teaching on the return of Christ and concurrent events is critically important. Hidden in these passages is a clearer view of Jesus—King of kings and Lord of lords—and a vivid picture of His bride, the victorious end-time church. Rather than feeling overwhelmed or unqualified to understand the meaning of it all, we can trust God give us eyes to see His Son and His bride as they really are!

CHAPTER 13

SCHOLARS WITH BURNING HEARTS

A Form of Godliness that Denies His Power (see II Timothy 3:5).

The Western church experienced a great move of God *and* a great test of faith in the 19th century. The Second Great Awakening brought in a harvest of hundreds of thousands of souls, *and* rising liberal theology caused hundreds of thousands to turn away from the faith. Immanuel Kant's atheistic philosophy of "enlightenment" had paved the way for Friedrich Schleiermacher and scores of liberal theologians after him to call the veracity Scripture into question. Soon, an entire movement of pseudo-Christianity denied biblical inerrancy, the virgin birth, Christ's divinity, His miracles, and every statement in the Bible that cannot be empirically proven. A generation raised with a biblical worldview began to fall away from the faith.

By 1900, a full-blown war was waging. Fundamentalists were confronting liberals head-on. Evangelicals rejected both the humanistic atheism of liberals and the legalism of the fundamentalists. Seminaries were the most strategic battlefields, and they were nearly all falling to liberal theology. The very training centers for church leadership—created to be bastions of truth and biblical clarity—began training would-be pastors to deny the uniqueness of Christ and authority of Scripture. It was during the early to mid-20th century that many mainline denominational seminaries were lost to doctrines of demons.

George Eldon Ladd

God was not willing to allow Christian academia to fall from the faith unchallenged. Fundamentalist and evangelical seminaries began cropping up throughout the United States. Dallas Theological Seminary and Fuller Theological Seminary were two of these, which are still going strong today. As we briefly discussed in chapter 2, George Eldon Ladd played a critical role during this historic juncture. In John A. D'Elia's excellent biography, *A Place at the Table*, he outlines how Ladd dedicated his life to infiltrating mainline, liberal academia with evangelical and Spirit-inspired scholarship. For nearly twenty years, Ladd labored to further his education and overcome seminarial roadblocks and obstacles intended to inhibit evangelical influence. Eventually, he completed a Ph.D. at Harvard and began producing some of the most powerful theological works of the 20th century.

In 1950 Ladd became the professor of Biblical Theology at Fuller, where he remained for the rest of his career. He played an enormous role in helping to establish the foundations and direction of the seminary. Ladd's works, *The Presence of the Future*, *A Theology of the New Testament*, *Jesus and the Kingdom*, and others have played a critical role in forming the theology of many of the most powerful ministries on earth today. His teachings on "Inaugurated Eschatology" and the "Already, Not Yet" perspective of the kingdom of God can be heard in the messages of thousands of modern men and women of God, whether or not they have ever read Ladd. John Wimber writes in *Kingdom Come*:

*At Fuller I was introduced to the writings of George Eldon Ladd, especially his books **The Presence of the Future** and **Critical Questions about the Kingdom of God**. From Dr. Ladd I came to believe that the kingdom of God is, in fact, relevant to our lives today. As I read George Ladd's books and reread the Gospels, I realized that at the very heart of THE GOSPEL lies the kingdom of God and that power for effective evangelism and discipleship relates directly to our understanding and experiencing the kingdom today. This revelation remains the most significant spiritual experience since my conversion in 1963, because thereafter I explored the practical implications of the presence of the kingdom.*

Kicking The Hornet's Nest

Ladd's mission to infiltrate academia advanced in spite of **"many adversaries" (see I Corinthians 16:9).** He underwent a great struggle to have his works distributed by predominately liberal academic publishers. There were also vocal critics downplaying Ladd's work as though an evangelical was incapable of producing quality scholarship. This criticism took a great toll on Ladd, affecting his emotional health, thus damaging his marriage and relationship with his children. On one occasion Norman Perrin, a liberal theologian, published a particularly negative review of Ladd's book, *Jesus and the Kingdom*, and Ladd was utterly crushed by it. He began to call himself a "scholarly wipeout" and his vision to break into mainstream academia, "a fools dream." According to John D'Elia and other historical accounts, Ladd never fully recovered from this onslaught of criticism. D'Elia thoroughly describes Ladd's downward spiral of "emotional, physical, and spiritual disintegration" over the next decade.

Why was this criticism so devastating to Ladd? Could a man who labored and fought forty years for his destiny have been so frail? It is more likely that Ladd unknowingly bumped up against a major satanic stronghold and he was unprepared for the backlash. History records no army of intercessors strategically praying for Ladd as his writings stirred up a hornet's nest of spiritual warfare. Ladd was a Spirit-filled and anointed man of God who devoted his life to infiltrating academia. He was storming the gates of the very seminaries that were dispensing the most deceptive pseudo-theologies into the church. There was significant demonic backlash aimed at Ladd and his family and it is quite possible he did not see it coming.

George Eldon Ladd's life and ministry are of great historic significance. A poll conducted by Mark Noll, author of *The Scandal of the Evangelical Mind*, once found Ladd's *A Theology of the New Testament* to be the second most influential book among evangelical scholars, second only to *Calvin's Institutes*. Ladd's work looms tall as a beacon of light in the midst of a dark time in church history. Is the world of Christian scholarship much brighter today? Where are the G.E. Ladd's of our generation—those Spirit-filled believers who will devote their lives to the pursuit of sound doctrine? Who will devote their whole lives to the "Scriptures and the power of God" (see Matthew 22:29)?

Do Not Be Deceived

The New Testament's predominant warning to the end-time church is, "Do not be deceived." In the "Olivet Discourse" as Jesus describes "the signs of his coming and of the end of the age," He exhorts **"see that no one leads you astray" (see Matthew 24:4).** Paul explicitly warns believers in the last days **"let no one deceive you" (see II Thessalonians 2:3).** He tells Timothy that at the time of the end, **"evil people and impostors will go on from bad to worse, deceiving and being deceived" (see II Timothy 3:13).** In Revelation, the beast's primary persuasive power is deception. The false prophet, or "the other beast," deceives the nations with false signs and wonders and demonically empowered words, directing them to follow the beast (see Revelation 13:14, 20:8).

In light of these warnings, we must know and contend for the truth. We must be prepared for the proliferation of false teachings and "doctrines of demons" that Paul and Peter prophesied for the time of the end (see I Timothy 4:1; II Peter 2:1). Deception and false teaching will rise from the kingdom of darkness with "lying signs and wonders." How will God's people respond?

We, the church, must become the kind of believers that God Himself is looking for. Jesus speaks of a future day in John 4:23, **"when the true worshipers will worship the Father in spirit and truth; for the Father is seeking such to worship Him."** The implications of this verse are stunning. The Father is actually seeking worshippers who are in pursuit of both the Spirit *and* the truth. There is a special access to God's heart for those that determine to grow in relationship with Holy Spirit *and* our understanding of the Word. We are called to be people of incredible strength and depth in the Scriptures *and* phenomenal power and authority in the Holy Spirit.

May we never again be satisfied in "having a form of godliness but denying its power." We cannot settle for a brand of Christianity that has no manifestation of the power of the Holy Spirit. Nor can we be content to experience the gifts and power of the Spirit while remaining shallow in His Word. It is essential that our pursuit of the supernatural be guided and fueled by Scripture. This is how we become people of the Word and the Spirit—those the Father is seeking. This is how we will become the victorious end-time church, who will confront and overcome end-time deception.

Scholars with Burning Hearts

The pursuit of true theology is the pursuit of the knowledge of God. Theology or *Theos-Logos* simply refers to words, thoughts, and understanding (*logos*) about God (*Theos*). The biblical idea of "the knowledge of God" is far more than head knowledge "about" God. Hosea's exhortation, **"Let us know, let us pursue the knowledge of the LORD" (see Hosea 6:3)** is meant to provoke us to spiritual hunger. This prophetic utterance is a call to know God personally and intimately. In the same passage, Hosea encourages, **"Let us return to the LORD . . . He will heal us . . . He will revive us . . . He will raise us up that we may live in His sight. Let us know, let us pursue the knowledge of the LORD. His going forth is established as the morning; He will come to us like the rain, like the latter and former rain to the earth" (Hosea 6:1-3).** These are the words of a hungry heart, desperate for God's presence—desperate to know Him. When we approach God with such a hungry heart, His presence will come and rain on us as surely as the sun rises in the morning.

If theology does not cause us to hunger and thirst for God, something is "off." Either the theology is merely "head knowledge" or we are approaching it as a purely intellectual exercise. Life-giving theology has the potential to light our hearts on fire with love for Jesus, to awaken passion for Him. God desires to raise up a multitude of scholars with burning hearts in our generation—students of the Word and the Spirit who are falling more and more in love with Him. These anointed teachers will help to shape the hearts and minds of a generation as they prepare for the coming of the Lord. Perhaps you are called to be such a scholar with a burning heart.

CHAPTER 14

CONFRONTING END-TIME ERROR

Tares in the Wheat

T he year was 1830. The fire of the Second Great Awakening was blazing in the Northeast. Charles Finney was five years into his western New York revival campaign. God was moving and the spiritual fervor of the people was at a fever pitch. The same year, in the same part of New York State, a young man named Joseph Smith published a book of "revelations" he had allegedly received through visions and angelic visitations: *The Book of Mormon.*

The rest is history. A cultish sect was born in the middle of a great awakening. "Multitudes, multitudes *were* in the valley of decision" (see Joel 3:14) and the enemy sought opportunity to ensnare the hearts of the undiscerning. The first-century Apostle Paul warned of precisely this kind of deception, **"Even if we, or an angel from heaven, preach any other gospel to you than what we have preached to you, let him be accursed" (Galatians 1:8).**

Jude 1:4 cautions us against false teachers who creep in "unnoticed" in the midst of our Christian fellowship to pervert

Scripture and deny the truth about Jesus. The Lord Himself exposed the satanic strategy to infiltrate God's end-time harvest in Matthew 13:25 **"While men slept, his enemy came and sowed tares among the wheat and went his way."** When God is moving, we must be more on guard than ever against false teachers and doctrines of demons. "Tares" of deception can be sown among revival "wheat."

Flies in the Ointment

Ecclesiastes 10:1 warns that a little dead fly will putrefy the fragrance of an entire bottle of perfume. In the same way a "little" lie can defile an entire doctrine. The trouble with deception is that it usually comes packaged in truth. In the example above, Mormons revere the Bible as one of their four "holy books." They conclude, however, that Adam and Eve moved to Jackson County, Missouri after being driven from the Garden of Eden.

Many of the errors being promoted in Christian circles today are packaged complete with Bible verses. These errors are often preached by people who seem to really know God. Their fragrance may be pleasant, and quite familiar, but something is "off" in the aroma.

As the Apostle Paul prepared Timothy by charging him to be strong and unwavering, our generation must do the same:

> **I charge you therefore before God and the Lord Jesus Christ, who will judge the living and the dead at His appearing and His kingdom:**
> **Preach the word! Be ready in season and out of season. Convince, rebuke, exhort, with all longsuffering and teaching.**

> **For the time will come when they will not endure sound doctrine, but according to their own desires, because they have itching ears, they will heap up for themselves teachers;**
>
> **and they will turn their ears away from the truth, and be turned aside to fables.**
>
> **But you be watchful in all things (see II Timothy 4:1-5).**

As we saw in the last chapter, God is relentless in warning against end-time deception. As we approach the end of this age, we must be relentless in our pursuit of truth and when necessary, our outcry against error. We must understand and be able to refute false teaching. Let's conclude our survey of the last days by identifying some of the potentially harmful false teachings being promoted in our day.

The Judgment of God

Understanding God's judgment is paramount to understanding His plan for the end of the age. Therefore, the enemy has labored to put forth many misconceptions and deceptive doctrines centered on this topic. We will expose several of them below.

Many in our day are calling into question the validity of the Old Testament. Some popular teachers reject large portions of Scripture because they contain commands to Israel like I Samuel 15:3, **"Now go and attack Amalek, and utterly destroy all that they have, and do not spare them. But kill both man and woman, infant and nursing child, ox and sheep, camel and donkey."** Many understandably find it offensive that God would require Israel to kill woman and children.

Some have flatly rejected the command to destroy Amalek and other judgment passages as being "uninspired" or only man's recollection of history and not really God's Word. The problem with this theory is the Scriptures make countless claims of Divine authorship (see Exodus 4:30; Joshua 3:9; Isaiah 34:16). We also have endless manuscript evidence to establish beyond a doubt that the Old Testament we have today is the exact same Old Testament that Jesus and the apostles used. The Dead Sea Scrolls provide some of the greatest assurances of this. Those copies of Scripture match our modern Bibles almost flawlessly.

There are several plausible reasons that God gave this command to annihilate Amalek. To name a few:

1. God had given Amalek many years to repent, but their evil had reached a fever pitch of child sacrifice, immorality, and idolatry. It was His mercy to allow children to be killed before they were old enough to participate in such wickedness and thus be eternally damned.

2. It is possible that the genealogy of Amalek had been corrupted with Nephilim DNA, as in Genesis 6. Deuteronomy 3:11 leaves open the possibility of Nephilim existing during this time. God wiped out the entire earth with a flood because of the extreme evil and corruption of the Nephilim once before.

3. Amalek had previously ambushed Israel from behind after they crossed the Red Sea and God vowed to utterly destroy them (see Deuteronomy 25:17-19).

The de facto issue at stake in the rejection of such verses as I Samuel 15:3 is the sovereignty of God. Whatever reasons God has for doing what He does—He is God. He does not have to answer to man, explain Himself to us, or justify His actions. This is the topic of Romans 9:13-24, where Paul is. that God does what God wants to do, whether or not manki.. understands or agrees with Him. We must bow to the Sovereign of the universe. Then we will be positioned to see what Paul saw as He bowed before God's sovereignty in Romans 11. Then, we will join his worship cry, **"Oh, the depth of the riches both of the wisdom and knowledge of God! How unsearchable are His judgments and His ways past finding out!"**

What do We Affirm?

There are other battlegrounds in this war over the judgment of God. Foremost is the debate over the appropriate Christian response to homosexuality. Many consider themselves Christians while living an ongoing, unrepentant gay lifestyle. Some churches now label themselves as "affirming"—or accepting of practicing homosexuality as a viable option for Christians. Such congregations would consider it judgmental, unloving, or hateful to challenge a person with the biblical standard—that a gay lifestyle is no more compatible with following Jesus than a lifestyle of adultery.

God's judgment on this matter is abundantly clear. I Corinthians 6:9 tells us that homosexuals and sodomites have no inheritance in the kingdom of God. Romans 1:26-27 tells us that homosexuality is vile, unnatural, shameful, erroneous, and deserving of penalty. Leviticus 18:22 calls homosexuality an "abomination." Nevertheless, many now demand that we interpret these and other crystal-clear passages in a convoluted way that deems homosexuality as a perfectly acceptable Christian lifestyle.

God loves LGBT men and women unconditionally, as much as everyone else on earth—and so should we. In the case of a Christian who is struggling and seeking freedom from homosexual sin or an LGBT person who is an unbeliever, we are called to welcome them into the church and offer the Good News of the Gospel. However, when someone claims to be a Christian and is an unrepentant homosexual, we are told, **"not to keep company"** with them, **"not even to eat with such a person" (see I Corinthians 5:9-13).** These truths invalidate so-called "affirming" churches as something other than a biblical church.

Our commitment to follow the dictates of Scripture must not stifle our compassion. In this fallen world, a person may actually be born with same-sex attraction. Likewise, others are born with a bent toward alcoholism or drug addiction. This may be a result of generational iniquity or the result of a demonic assignment against a person's life. The relevant question is: does a congenital predisposition towards addiction or same-sex attraction exempt someone from God's standards of righteousness? Are such people just as responsible to fight against the lust of the flesh as every other believer? The conspicuous answer is "yes."

Based on the prenatal factors above, some people may have a greater challenge in resisting temptation than others. However, the man or woman struggling with anger, gluttony, or covetousness may protest that they are in the greatest battle of their lives—even if their sin is less scandalous. As Kris Vallotton has said, "You know the most intense temptation in the world? The one you struggle with." Therefore, we must approach every struggling person with compassion, gentleness, and a desire to see them restored (see Galatians 6:1). Sin is sin and we dare not compromise God's definition of morality nor condemn any who are repentant and seeking to be free.

Judging His Judgments

As mentioned above, proper perspective on God's judgment is an indispensable aid in understanding the end times. It is no coincidence that many of the major current controversies center on this issue. It seems that Daniel spoke of the two controversies above nearly two thousand six hundred years ago when he prophesied that the antichrist will **"regard neither the God of his fathers nor the desire of women" (see Daniel 11:37).** The spirit of antichrist has a calculated agenda to trivialize the majesty of God and the authority of Scripture and to promote homosexuality. We can expect that these two battlegrounds will be contested until the very end.

The pressure to conform to the morality of culture will remain. Mankind will continually insist that their ways are higher than God's ways—their judgments are true and His are unjust. God's answer from heaven is clear: **"Would you indeed annul My judgment? Would you condemn Me that you may be justified?" (Job 40:8).** Thousands of years after God originally spoke these words to Job, mankind still seeks to *condemn God* and *annul His judgment in order to justify ourselves.*

"There is only one Lawgiver and Judge" (see James 4:12 NASB) and it is the ultimate arrogance of man to pass judgment on His judgments. The definition of righteousness belongs to Him and Him alone (see Daniel 9:7). He is the only one qualified to define right and wrong, truth and error, and we must bow before His judgments. God enlightens us in Isaiah 55:8-9, **"For My thoughts are not your thoughts, nor are your ways My ways," says the LORD. "For as the heavens are higher than the earth, so are My ways higher than your ways, and My thoughts than your thoughts."** Amen.

MSU
MORNINGSTAR UNIVERSITY

MorningStar University is for those seeking to live a high-impact life of unrelenting pursuit of the high calling to serve the King of kings with the devotion He deserves. The greatest leaders are also the greatest followers of Christ, and that is our curriculum. The true Christian life is the greatest adventure we can ever live, and it's also a life of impact like no other. If this is your resolve, MorningStar University may be for you.

WWW.MORNINGSTARUNIVERSITY.COM

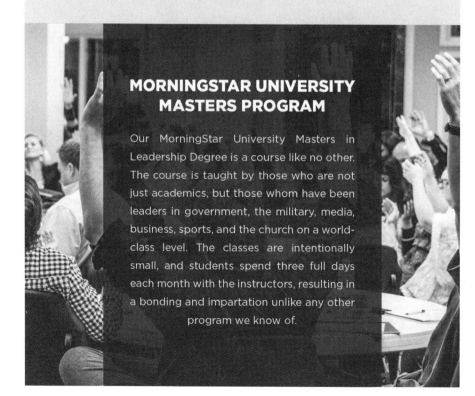

MORNINGSTAR UNIVERSITY MASTERS PROGRAM

Our MorningStar University Masters in Leadership Degree is a course like no other. The course is taught by those who are not just academics, but those whom have been leaders in government, the military, media, business, sports, and the church on a world-class level. The classes are intentionally small, and students spend three full days each month with the instructors, resulting in a bonding and impartation unlike any other program we know of.

PARTNERS

Our MorningStar Partners have grown into an extraordinary global fellowship of men and women who are committed to seeing The Great Commission fulfilled in our times. Join us in equipping the body of Christ through conferences, schools, media, and publications.

We are committed to multiplying the impact of the resources entrusted to us. Your regular contribution of any amount—whether it's once a month or once a year—will make a difference!

In His Service,

PARTNER WITH US TODAY

MORNINGSTAR
WORSHIP

STREAMING ON

 |  Spotify | TRIBL

FOLLOW US

 MORNINGSTAR.WORSHIP

WWW.MORNINGSTARWORSHIP.COM

ABOUT THE AUTHOR

Justin Perry is the Lead Pastor of MorningStar Fellowship Church in Fort Mill, SC. After a dramatic salvation experience in 2000, Justin began spending many hours a day in the presence of God and the study of His Word. He almost immediately began to walk in supernatural ministry, demonstrating and equipping the body of Christ in healing, prophetic ministry, and evangelism. Justin has a passion for the church to know the Scriptures and the power of God. Whether training in the gifts of the Spirit or teaching Systematic Theology, he makes daunting and complicated issues inviting and accessible. Justin is the author of several other books, including *Adventures in Dreaming: The Supernatural Nature of Dreams,* and T*rue Theology Vol. I: Encountering the Knowledge of God.* He and his wife, LeeAnna, have two sons and a daughter and live in Fort Mill, SC.